The Madcap Christian Scientist's Middle Book:
Further Adventures in Christian Science
By Karen Molenaar Terrell

Copyright 2012 Karen Molenaar Terrell
All right reserved.

ISBN-10:1477442456
ISBN-13:978-1477442456

(cover photo by Karen Molenaar Terrell)

For Andrew, Alexander, and Scott,
and all the other wonderful family members and friends
in my community
who helped lift me up during my Middle Book -
with much love, appreciation, and gratitude -
thank you.

The power of a moment
Each one ripe with possibilities
Each one bringing the opportunity
of the first meeting of a new friend,
a new insight, a cessation
of pain, a sweet kiss, a lark's trill,
a glimmer of light on water,
a precious memory…

--Karen Molenaar Terrell

Introduction

"WILDERNESS. Loneliness; doubt; darkness; Spontaneity of thought and idea; the vestibule in which a material sense of things disappears, and spiritual sense unfolds the great facts of existence." –
from *Science and Health with Key to the Scriptures* by Mary Baker Eddy

"...And we know that all things work together for good to them that love God..."
– Romans 8: 28

"But this is one of his clouded times and He'll out of 'em enough to shake the tree Of life itself and bring down fruit unheard of..."
– Edwin Arlington Robinson

***

My son and I recently talked about my previous book, *Blessings: Adventures of a Madcap Christian Scientist*. I told him that book was true for the person I was then, and I'm glad I wrote it, but I couldn't write the same book now. Andrew told me I should write another book then, for this time in my life. I told him that my recent life experience has been kind of dark. He said I should write about *that* then, and he started talking about trilogies – how almost every life story has three parts – the first book is usually happy and innocent, the second one is dark and challenging, and the last book is the triumph book. Andrew said it was time for me to write "the middle book." He assures me the book about the golden years will come, but he says that book can't come until the middle book gets written.

So what you see here is me sucking it up and writing The Middle Book.

I need to write The Middle Book quickly, though, because I already see the golden years glimmering just beyond each word I type, and I can see the dark rapidly being replaced by the dawn. I'm sitting here, shaking my head in faux exasperation. This is just so typical. I never seem to be able to hold off my happy endings for any great length of time. I can see now that, even if I was determined to stay in The Middle Book, Life wouldn't let me. As Mary Baker Eddy says in *Science and Health with Key to the Scriptures,* "…progress is the law of God, whose law demands of us only what we can certainly fulfill."

My hope is that by sharing my own Middle Book story, those who are just now entering *their* Middle Book will be relieved to discover they're not alone, and before long *they'll* see the dawn begin to lift the darkness, too. We're all in this together…

A Merry Heart

"A merry heart doeth good like a medicine..." –
Proverbs 17: 22

"Mentally contradict every complaint from the body, and rise to the true consciousness of Life as Love, - as all that is pure, and bearing the fruits of Spirit... Hatred, envy, dishonesty, fear, and so forth, make a man sick, and neither material medicine nor Mind can help him permanently, even in body, unless it makes him better mentally, and so delivers him from his destroyers... Christian Science practice begins with Christ's keynote of harmony, 'Be not afraid!'"
– Mary Baker Eddy

"Against the assault of laughter, nothing can stand."
– Mark Twain

***

I am a goof. But I have learned to take advantage of this, and the laughter that my goofiness has brought on, has also brought a lot of healing with it.

There was the time, for instance, when I noted how dusty my silk wall-hanging from India had become and, knowing it would be ruined it if I tried to wash it, I thought it would be a fine idea to take it out to the back porch and shake it out. This wall-hanging had little beads all around the top and the bottom of it, and, when I gave it a good whap, one of the beads flapped up and hit me right in the middle of my forehead.

It hurt. But it was also so dang funny that I found myself doubled-over, laughing and crying simultaneously, while a goose egg started growing on my forehead.

My husband, Scott, heard me laughing, and came out to see what scrape I'd gotten myself into *this* time. When he saw the goose egg on my forehead, he observed, "Looks like you've got the mark of the beast there," and then went back inside to finish doing whatever it was he'd been doing. His comment brought on a renewed fit of laughter.

The bump on my forehead was pretty large, but it was impossible to take the whole ridiculous incident at all seriously – and that, I believe, is the key to why the bump soon went down, leaving no sign of injury. I simply did not have it in me to give any of it any reality or power. It was like it was all a part of some Lucille Ball or Groucho Marx skit.

Laughter is good medicine.

***

Several years ago I went to my optometrist for my annual check-up. While he was looking at my eyes through a magnifying lens, he got kind of quiet, and then told me that he saw a melanoma on one of my eyelids. He took a picture of it, and pointed out the melanoma to me. He told me he'd like me to make an appointment right then, from his office, with a specialist.

His receptionist called the office of a local eye surgeon, and put me on the phone to talk with the surgeon's receptionist, to make an appointment.

I was at my comedic best.

I can't remember now, exactly, what I said to the dear lady – but I had her laughing, and I was cracking myself up, too, and when the doctor walked in and heard me chatting away to the surgeon's receptionist, he started smiling. "Tell her you're not ready to start ordering caskets, yet," he said. Which only made me crack up even more. Whatever mesmeric fear might have been forming in my thoughts, disappeared in the laughter.

As I walked out the door of the optometrist's office, I was completely filled with a sense of peace and confidence, and a comforting voice filled my thoughts: "Fear not. You are my precious child."

The appointment with the eye surgeon wasn't for a couple weeks, and during that time I diligently studied *The Bible* and the Christian Science textbook, *Science and Health with Key to the Scriptures*, to get a better sense of my identity as God's "precious child" and a better understanding of my Father-Mother God, Love. In *Science and Health*, Mary Baker Eddy instructs us: "'Agree to disagree' with approaching symptoms of chronic or acute disease, whether it is cancer, consumption, or smallpox. Meet the incipient stages of disease with as powerful mental opposition as a legislator would employ to defeat the passage of an inhuman law. Rise in the conscious strength of the spirit of Truth to overthrow the plea of mortal mind…"

When the time came to drive into the doctor's office for my appointment, I had no sense of fear at all. I knew I was safe and dwelling in the consciousness of Love – never separated from Love – wholly pure and untouched by anything unlike God, Good. I knew there was "no spot where God is not."

The eye surgeon began to look at my eyelid through a magnifying lens. He didn't see anything at all that resembled a melanoma. He pulled down a stronger magnifying lens, and then an even stronger one. He saw nothing. He asked me which eyelid it was – thinking maybe he was looking at the wrong one, I guess. But he never found anything that looked like a melanoma. He finally clipped a piece of skin from my eyelid to send in for analysis. But he let me know that he'd seen nothing at all alarming on my skin.

When the results of the biopsy came back, there was no indication of melanoma.

***

Two years ago I woke up to discover my right hand had swelled up to twice its normal size. It was really weird. My fingers were so puffed-up I couldn't bend them, and my hand was throbbing with pain.

When I went into work, everyone who saw my hand began telling me their horror stories – a bad allergic reaction that almost killed a son, infections gone awry – stuff like that. I was advised to go see a doctor immediately, and I have to admit, by the time I'd heard everyone's dramatic life-and-death stories, I was a little scared.

When I got to the doctor's office, he told me it was probably a serious infection or rheumatoid arthritis – although my case, he said, was atypical of either one of those because my joints weren't inflamed and I had no open wounds. The doctor told me he wanted to get my blood tested, and in the meantime he recommended that I get myself shot full of all kinds of drugs that would take care of both an infection and an inflammation. I told him I didn't want any drugs – at least not until I knew more what was going on – but I did agree to get my blood tested. So I did that. And then I went home and called a Christian Science practitioner for prayerful support. The confidence and assurance I heard in the practitioner's voice as I talked to her was a great help to me, mentally, and she agreed to pray with me.

One of the things I needed to handle in my thoughts was the fear that I'd allowed to fill them. In *Science and Health with Key to the Scriptures,* Mary Baker Eddy writes, "Fear, which is an element of all disease, must be cast out to readjust the balance for God... Take possession of your body, and govern its feeling and action. Rise in the strength of Spirit to resist all that is unlike good. God has made man capable of this, and nothing can vitiate the ability and power divinely bestowed on man... Have no fear that matter can ache, swell, and be inflamed as the result of a law of any kind, when it is self-evident that matter can have no pain nor inflammation...Matter cannot be inflamed. Inflammation is fear, an excited state of mortals which is not normal."

When I woke up the next morning, my hand appeared to be even more swollen, but mentally I wasn't filled with fear, anymore. I called the practitioner again, and she agreed to continue praying for me. When I woke up on the second morning, I woke up healed – the pain was gone, and I could once again bend my fingers and had complete freedom of movement, and the puffiness had almost entirely disappeared.

I called the doctor's office to find out if they'd gotten back the results of the blood test, and was told that the results indicated there was something wrong. The doctor wanted me to come in and talk to him. I told the receptionist that I was actually completely fine. She was surprised to hear this and brought a nurse to the phone. The nurse told me that one of the markers for rheumatoid arthritis was high, and the doctor wanted to refer me to a rheumatoid arthritis specialist. I told her I was actually doing great, and she was glad to hear this. She told me they wouldn't go any further right now. I asked her to tell the doctor that I'd called a Christian Science practitioner to help me and had gotten better after that. I thought he might get a kick out of that – I'm pretty sure the doctor already thinks I'm kind of "weird" – in a good way, of course.

When I went to work that morning, I was all excited to show all the people who had predicted dire consequences for me, how quickly my hand had deflated, and to share with them how the healing had come about for me. But what I found interesting was that none of the people who had been so adamant about the dangers and seriousness of my recently-inflamed hand seemed to even remember that it had ever been puffed-up, or seemed in the least surprised that it no longer was.

And maybe that's as it should be.

***

Healing in Christian Science is a very natural thing – it's not supernatural, but supremely natural – it's not a miracle, but a natural manifestation of Truth.

In her book, *Science and Health with Key to the Scriptures*, Mary Baker Eddy defines "MIRACLE" as "That which is divinely natural, but must be learned humanly; a phenomenon of Science." Eddy writes, "A miracle fulfills God's law, but does not violate that law…" and she says, "Now, as then (in Jesus' time), these mighty works (healings) are not supernatural, but supremely natural…We must learn that evil is the awful deception and unreality of existence. Evil is not supreme; good is not helpless; nor are the so-called laws of matter primary, and the law of Spirit secondary."

Scientific research has shown that certain emotions – the negative emotions of worry and sadness, and the positive emotions of happiness and enjoyment, for instance - can have a huge affect on a person's physical well-being.

On the *ScienceDaily* website (March 4, 2009) in an article entitled *Human Emotions Hold Sway Over Physical Health Worldwide*, we're told: "The research proves that positive emotions are critical for upkeep of physical health for people worldwide…" and "…positive emotions unmistakably are linked to better health, even when taking into account a lack of basic needs."
(http://www.sciencedaily.com/releases/2009/03/090304091229.htm)

I think this research correlates well to the healings and teachings found in Christian Science – a way of life that includes the belief that our state of mind determines our human experience.

I know this way of looking at life may seem really foreign and odd to most people. I've heard people say that they don't want to bother God with their insignificant little problems when God has so many other things to worry about, and I know most people today probably turn to traditional medical science first for their physical problems, and think it's strange to question that, or to do anything else.

I guess I just have a different perspective on this stuff. From my perspective it's not an imposition on God to expect Her to be God. How can it be an imposition on Love to be Love, or on Truth to be Truth? When I "pray" about a situation, I'm not pleading with God to fix everything, or imposing on God's time or anything. When I pray I'm trying to bring my thoughts into harmony with Love. I'm not asking God to do anything different than She's already doing. God is, for me, constant, unchanging Love – and it's my responsibility to align myself with Her, to recognize myself as Her idea, made in Her image, without blemish, discord, or fear. I have found that when I'm able to do this, I experience healing.

***

You probably all know the story of Norman Cousins, a long-time editor at the *Saturday Review*, who, upon being told by medical doctors that he had a fatal and incurable disease, plied himself with Marx Brothers movies for a month, and returned to the doctors, cured of his disease. He wrote a book about his experiences called *Anatomy of an Illness*, which went on to become a best-seller. I am firmly convinced that Norman Cousins and I would have hit it off famously, had we ever met.

I have found that laughter and a "merry heart" really ARE the best medicine.

Insanity

"The treatment of insanity is especially interesting. However obstinate the case, it yields more readily than do most diseases to the salutary action of truth, which counteracts error. The arguments to be used in curing insanity are the same as in other diseases: namely, the impossibility that matter, brain, can control or derange mind, can suffer or cause suffering; also the fact that truth and love will establish a healthy state, guide and govern mortal mind or the thought of the patient, and destroy all error, whether it is called dementia, hatred, or any other discord." – Mary Baker Eddy

"Character cannot be developed in ease and quiet. Only through experience of trial and suffering can the soul be strengthened, ambition inspired, and success achieved."
– Helen Keller

"Sometimes you have to lose your mind to come to your senses."
– from *The Peaceful Warrior* by Dan Millman

***

At the age of 51 I went insane. I did not like it so much. But I learned a lot from it.

Eckhart Tolle tells us: "Life will give you whatever experience is most helpful for the evolution of your consciousness." He asks, "How do you know this is the experience you need? Because," he says, "this is the experience you are having at this moment." I really like how he puts that. My thought is that something is only a challenge to us when there's a lesson to learn from it. Two people, in other words, might find themselves in identical situations – and one of those people might coast through the situation, and the other might stumble through it – depending on where each individual is in her spiritual progress.

I did a lot of stumbling during The Year of Insanity, and I learned a whole lot of lessons. It was, in essence, my last hurrah – my final experience with the lessons of "callow youth" and ego, before I could move on to the next stage in my development.

During The Year of Insanity it seemed I was confronted with temptation at every turn. I had to come face-to-face with ego, vanity, pride, insecurity, and addiction to praise. It was a really difficult time for me. It felt like I was at the bottom of a deep, dark pit, and I didn't know how I was going to get out of there. I lost weight, couldn't sleep, had a constant dialogue going on inside my head about the past and the future, had to keep moving – trying to get away from myself, I guess – and had an actual physical heartache from the sadness I felt. There were times when I just wanted to hide myself away from the world, and not have to deal with this stuff anymore. There were times when I was so full of guilt about the feelings I was having that I just wanted to kill myself, and be done with it. There was a constant battle going on inside me, and it was really wearing.

If somebody had tried to talk to me about mental illness before I'd had this experience, I wouldn't have had a clue what they were going on about. Mental illness was something that happened to "other" people. Mental illness was not something a madcap Christian Scientist would ever know anything about, right?

Yeesh.

I might have chosen, with good reason, to seek professional help during this time. I might have chosen, again with good reason, to take anti-depressant medications. And after having been through this experience, I can tell you – without any hesitation – that I do not fault anyone, at all, for seeking professional help and using medication if they think it'll help them get through the kind of thing I went through during that year. And I can also understand why it might be hard for people to cogitate why I *didn't* do those things in an effort to help myself.

All I can tell you, really, is that there was some part of me that felt I needed this experience – that I needed to feel the full depth and breadth of it – and there was a part of me that believed if I could survive this, I would come out of it much wiser and stronger than before I went into it. I guess I calculated the costs and rewards and decided the rewards would be worth it. If I could survive.

I give credit to Christian Science, and to my Father-Mother God, for getting me through this time. I absolutely know I wouldn't have been able to make it without the understanding of God, Good, I'd gained through my study of Christian Science.

I also need to give thanks to three authors whose writings meant a great deal to me while I was working my way through that year. I've already quoted one of them – Eckhart Tolle - a contemporary thinker who's had his own experience with depression, and has generously shared his wisdom and insights about that in several recent best-sellers. The second of the three authors was a liberal Christian minister of the late 1800's named Henry Drummond. His book, *The Greatest Thing in the World*, was chock full of wise and wonderful thoughts on love – "the greatest thing in the world." The third author was a man named Edward A. Kimball, an inspiring and mentally-rousing Christian Science lecturer and teacher during the late 1800's and early 1900's.

Regarding my desire to hide myself away from temptation, Henry Drummond had this to say to me: "Above all, do not resent temptation; do not be perplexed because it seems to thicken round you more and more, and ceases neither for effort nor for agony nor prayer. That is your practice. That is the practice which God appoints you, and it is having its work in making you patient, and humble, and generous, and unselfish, and kind, and courteous." Drummond goes on to say: "Therefore keep in the midst of life. Do not isolate yourself. Be among men and among things, and among troubles, and difficulties, and obstacles… Talent develops itself in solitude - the talent of prayer, of faith, of meditation, of seeing the unseen; character grows in the stream of the world's life. That chiefly is where men are to learn love."

Drummond's admonition to "keep in the midst of life" was really helpful to me. His words helped me look at the challenges I was facing as blessings and needed lessons in my path towards progress, rather than as proof of my weakness, or a reason to feel guilty.

Edward A. Kimball, too, was helpful to me in dealing with the feelings of guilt that seemed to be a symptom of the depression. In his book, *Lectures and Articles on Christian Science*, Kimball writes, "It won't do you a particle of good to enter upon a career of self-condemnation. Remorse never got anybody into heaven. A sense of regret and all that sort of thing is not the process. The process is reform; it is change; it is correction..."

Kimball writes, "...a purely human giving up endeavor does not give up, but does involve the scientist in a sense of greater fear. Evil is never disposed of as though it were something. It cannot be given up as though it were something...Try to realize that through Christian Science, you are constantly gaining that which will do everything for you, and that you will succeed according to the gaining process."

This thought helped bring me peace – the insight that trying to fight an addiction by turning it into A Big Obstacle and using human will to force myself to "give it up" wasn't the way for me to be healed – but that I needed to fill up the holes and emptiness I felt in my life by gaining an understanding of what constitutes true happiness and filling my life up with that. As my friend, Sabra, pointed out to me, we don't remember the last time we laid down our dollies and moved on to other joys – giving up my toys was not a Major Event or something I had to force upon myself – it was a natural step in my forward way. And it can be that way with every forward step we take – we aren't so much "giving up" something, as we are gaining something.

Here's some of what I gained during this time: a new understanding and appreciation of love; a greater sense of gratitude for the power of a moment, and of a good, deep breath; a greater appreciation for choice; renewed gratitude for all the beauty in Nature and mankind; greater humility, empathy and compassion; and a greater commitment to my own spiritual journey. I'd entered The Year of Insanity an untested "youth" – gliding through life's challenges on a kind of cavalier, simple joy, without really having to put much work or effort into my mental frame of mind. By the time I exited that year I had a much deeper understanding of God, and who I am, as God's expression.

***

Dear Lord and Father of us all,
Forgive our foolish ways;
Reclothe us in our rightful mind;
In purer lives Thy service find,
In deeper reverence, praise.

Breathe through the pulses of desire
Thy coolness and Thy balm;
Let sense be dumb, let flesh retire;
Speak through the earthquake, wind and fire,
O still small voice of calm.

Drop Thy still dews of quietness,
Till all our strivings cease;
Take from us now the strain and stress,
And let our ordered lives confess
The beauty of Thy peace.

- John Greenleaf Whittier

Following the Crumbs Back to Myself

"So God created man in his own image, in the image of God created he him; male and female created he them." –
Genesis 1: 27

"The Scriptures inform us that man is made in the image and likeness of God... Man is spiritual and perfect; and because he is spiritual and perfect, he must be so understood in Christian Science. Man is idea, the image, of Love; he is not physique. He is the compound idea of God, including all right ideas... that which has no separate mind from God; that which has not a single quality underived from Deity..."
– Mary Baker Eddy

"You is kind. You is smart. You is important." –
From *The Help* by Kathryn Stockett

***

A few months after my fifty-first birthday, I no longer knew who I was. I don't mean I had amnesia or anything, but the person I'd always thought I was didn't seem to exist any longer. As my sons had become self-sufficient and independent young men, my role as their mother was different, and, as the only female in my family, I sometimes struggled with trying to figure out how I "fit in"; my profession had changed so much I no longer felt I belonged in it; and two close 20-year friendships, that had once defined who I was as a friend, had ended abruptly, leaving me feeling unworthy of friendship and unlovable. There were all at once a lot of holes in my life, and I felt like a loser.

Who the heck WAS I?

During the Year of Insanity I put a lot of thought into that question. Just when I'd start feeling like I was hopelessly lost in the wilderness, and would never find my way back to my real self, one of my fellow classmates in "Earth's preparatory school" (as Mary Baker Eddy described our time here) would drop a crumb on the forest floor that would help lead me the right direction. I don't think many of these classmates had any idea how important those crumbs were to me. So, to those of you who dropped the crumbs, I want to take a moment and tell you that you saved my life, and I whole-heartedly thank you for that.

Henry Drummond writes (in *The Greatest Thing in the World*): "The people who influence you are people who believe in you... To be trusted is to be saved. And if we try to influence or elevate others, we shall soon see that success is in proportion to their belief of our belief in them... It is when a man has no one to love him that he commits suicide. So long as he has friends, those who love him and whom he loves, he will live, because to live is to love... The withholding of love is the negation of the Spirit of Christ."

I have discovered, as I've lived my Middle Book, that I am over-the-top wealthy with friends. There have been times when I've felt my friends' expressions of Love towards me lifting me up and supporting me – giving me the buoyancy I need to stay afloat – and when I write "lifting me up" I mean that in a literal sense – I have felt myself – not my body, but my thoughts – literally rising.

I'd like to share a couple of instances with you of times when this happened for me – and I'd like to ask that as you read through these examples, you insert yourself into them – insert yourself as the person who is being shown love, and then insert yourself as the person who is showing love. Because, dear reader, the love that was expressed towards me is yours, too. You are the loved, and you are the loving.

***

One night during the depression, I got an encouraging call from my youngest brother, David, who had heard I was struggling. Near the end of our conversation, he said something that has stayed with me in the years since then. "Karen, did you ever see that movie with Tom Hanks where he gets stuck on the island?" Yes, I told him, I'd seen that movie. "For four years he was trying to get off that island," my brother said, "and then one day the tide brought in that piece of metal that he could use for a sail. He wasn't expecting it. He couldn't have known it was going to come in with the tide. But it saved him. You never know what the tide will bring in that will save you."

And, man, ain't that the truth? Just as I have found that there's no way I can predict what form help and "salvation" will take for me, I have found that, if I just keep my thought open to all the good that God offers us, every moment, I'll find everything I need to get me off my mental "island."

***

On New Year's Eve, 2007, I was hit particularly hard by the belief of depression – caught up in weird and intense feelings of hopelessness and worthlessness. I don't know what led me to check out my book on Amazon that night, but when I clicked on *Blessings: Adventures of a Madcap Christian Scientist* I found that just that day someone had added a new review for my book. The review read, in part: "Karen becomes your friend, someone you know and love and you know if she knew you, she would love you the way you want to be loved." I read those words and was so touched by them I began to cry. This was exactly the message I needed at that moment. If I could love others, I had worth. If others could love me, there was hope. I've always felt that the man who wrote that review had been listening to the voice of Love that day. He'd been guided by Love's direction to take the time to write a review for my book – and, because he did that for me, he helped to bring me out of a place of deep despair.

We all have access to an incredible power to bring good to other peoples' lives. That day my book's reviewer had tapped into that power.

***

My eldest son, Andrew, understood that I desperately needed to get away from "myself" – needed to get away from the routine of my life - and volunteered to go with me to the Oregon coast during our Spring Break. His willingness to accompany me on a fourteen-hour drive (round trip) meant a great deal to me and, frankly, surprised me. What sixteen year-old young man do *you* know who would volunteer to go with his mom on a road trip?

We had such a great time. We're both kind of easy-going when it comes to traveling. Sometimes I would wander, accidentally or on purpose, off the beaten track, and it would take me awhile to find my way back to our route – but Andrew never panicked about any of this. He just let me take him wherever I ended up going, without worry or concern about it. I remember one time we pulled over at a "scenic viewpoint" to find ourselves looking down on a sawmill and pulp mill that was belching up great plumes of smoke. Without saying a word, Andrew and I looked at each other and started snickering – I knew what he was thinking – scenic viewpoint?!

On the way down, we stopped to visit with my beloved Aunt Junie. Here's what I wrote in my journal about that visit: "Spent the night with Aunt Junie. She is so amazing. She's like Yoda. I was all weepy, told her I'd made mistakes and had lost close friends who told me I was a bad friend and a bad person. Junie was appalled. She said I am a good person – all her intuition tells her that I am a good person and she has no doubts about that."

Junie believed in me, had faith in me, and trusted in me. And I really needed that at the moment. She told me that "there are no unrightable wrongs, no unforgiveable sins, no fatal mistakes, no fatal diseases, only the eternal now." To be given hope and a fresh start is incredibly freeing.

***

I emailed my wise friend, David Allen, to get his thoughts on "identity" – he always has good stuff to share with me. I told him that I'd reached a point where I didn't know who I was, anymore – it felt like all my anchors were gone – my job wasn't the same job, my role as a mom wasn't the same role, I wasn't really a mountain-climber, anymore – who was I?! His response was one of the most profound pieces of writing I have ever read, and I'd like to share it with you:

"Karen, I know this feeling. A few years back, before I met you, I went through a similar experience. Up until that time I had identified as a completely self-reliant runner and professional designer who could succeed at anything I wanted to. That was me, or at least, that was who I thought was me. Suddenly, all that was gone...I felt like I had lost my entire identity...Then, one day it hit me. I am not any of those things. Those are things I do, not things that I am. Here is what I am: I am creative, curious, and kind. I like children and I like teaching. I enjoy physical activity. I am a storyteller and I like to make people laugh. I like to do things. I like to make things. I love to learn new things. And I love my family. Whether I am working or running, I am still all of those things. No matter what others may say or think, I am still all of those things. These are the things that never change. These are the things that make me, me. Sometimes I make mistakes and screw up, but that doesn't change any of those things, either. I am not always happy, but I am always grateful for the things that I am. And I don't worry anymore about the things I am not."

***

I'd met David on a religion discussion forum – he was a self-avowed atheist – but other than our difference in belief about God, we'd found we had a huge amount in common with each other. There were several other people I'd met on the forum – most of them atheists, like David – who had become valued friends to me. One of these valued friends was a brilliant wit named Jamie Longmire, who lived in Nova Scotia with his talented artist-wife, Kathi Petersen. Not long after I met Jamie, he "brought me home" via email to introduce me to Kathi.

Before too long Kathi and I were email buddies – emailing each other regularly twice a day. Kathi had been through some pretty major challenges in her life, and could relate to a lot of what I was going through. She understood my thoughts about not wanting to use medication to get relief from the depression – understood that I felt there was something I needed to learn from my experience. She understood, too, when I told her that I'd found I could be happy even when I was depressed. Kathi wrote:

> "...something... that occurs to me ... is that we all have to live our own lives, and grow from our own hardships.
>
> "I was in a Jungian dream group once and one of the women was saying something about how she could be just as conscious and psychologically grown without having had a dark night of the soul, and you could tell people were thinking 'yeah right' ... I hear peoples' stories sometimes, maybe some television interview, and they end up talking about their really pivotal growth 'dark night moment,' and it is something that seems so insignificant ...but you have to have the whole context of peoples' lives. I think it is hugely important for people to grow from their own experiences...

"I actually think in a way that it is very important not to tell someone, when they are upset about the bad time they are going through, 'Well look at that guy, he has no arms or legs and he is a professional motivational speaker and has written two bestseller books'... I'm saying this because I think in a way, the hardships (while all different) have a BIG sameness about them, and that the answers have a HUGE sameness about them. It is... about people who are suffering, and people finding out that the suffering isn't a necessary part of life. The hardships may be ... but the suffering not necessarily. I have thought that having bigger challenges can sometimes allow people to learn this more easily (trial by fire?) - to learn that life can be full of joy regardless ..."

***

I remember clearly the moment when I began to wake up from the depression: I was talking with my husband, Scott, about how the people around me were telling me these wonderful things about myself, but I just felt detached from their words – like the words had nothing to do with who I really am. I told him I felt like a fraud. He looked at me and started laughing. "Karen," he said, "everyone *else* knows who you are, you're the only one who can't see it!"

The way he said it – with such conviction and so kind of matter-of-factly – I felt something lifting from me, some burden that had been weighing me down. I went out for a walk, and everything around me looked lighter and brighter. I felt stirrings of joy. For some reason I'd been feeling like I had to "steal" happiness – as if I didn't deserve it. But I think that it was at this moment when I began to accept that I had every right to be happy.

***

"Be happy at all times and in all places; for remember it is right and a duty you owe to yourself and to your God to retain the right, no matter how loudly the senses scream." –
Edward A. Kimball

New Eyes

"Having eyes, see ye not?" – Mark 8: 18

"EYES. Spiritual discernment, - not material but mental." – Mary Baker Eddy

"...watch with glittering eyes the whole world around you because the greatest secrets are always hidden in the most unlikely places. Those who don't believe in magic will never find it." – Roald Dahl

***

So I was in kind of an interesting position. Things that I'd valued had been lost during The Year of Insanity, and there were new holes in my life that needed to be filled. I was curious to see how that would all work out for me.

One of the holes that needed to be filled was the hole that had been created by the loss of those two close friendships during TYofI, but those holes were almost immediately filled-in by new friendships, or by old friendships that moved from the back to the forefront of my life.

I've already mentioned three of the new friendships I found on the religion discussion forum – David Allen, Jamie Longmire, and Kathi Petersen. Even though I'd never met these people, or my other new friends from the religion forum, in person – their humor, wisdom, and friendship all became very important to me as I worked my way through TYoI and beyond. Kathi was the one who had actually recommended Eckhart Tolle's books to me. She was, and is, a very spiritually-minded person, and she and I also share a love for laughing, creating, and appreciating the beauty all around us.

Kathi is the reason I got back into photography in a big way, too. Because of her situation, I knew she would probably never be able to come out and visit my family and me in Bow, Washington. But I so wanted to share my part of the world with her. So I began to take photos of the beautiful things and people I saw on my walks – and, because she's an artist – I tried to take pictures worthy of someone with an artistic eye.

I began to look at my part of the world as Kathi might see it – as an artist and a tourist might see it – and this opened up a whole new awareness in me of the beauty around me. I felt like I was looking at everything with new eyes.

There was one afternoon, for instance, when I stepped outside my house for an afternoon "photo walk" and, with my "new eyes," I entered a world of awe and wonder. Trumpeter swans flew in the sky to the south of me, and a pair of bald eagles swooped around in the sky to the north of me, and I was just blown away by the magnificence of it. Totally oblivious to everything but those eagles and those trumpeters, I stood in the middle of the street, mouth open in wonder, focused on capturing what I was seeing in my camera.

I didn't realize that a car had stopped for me, and the driver was watching me in sort of amused fascination, until I finally took my eyes off the sky. Kind of embarrassed, but still full of the wonder of my world, I laughed and apologized for making him stop. The driver grinned back at me. He said I looked like I was really concentrating. Waving my arm towards the heavens, I said, "We live in a beautiful part of the world! – eagles and swans filling the sky!"

He smiled and kind of shrugged and said, "Nothing new."

I smiled back at him and said, "It's ALL new! I'm looking at the world with new eyes. I'm a tourist here."

He chuckled. I think he thought I was a little daft. And perhaps I was, and am – but I'm sure enjoying this new awareness of my surroundings, and my new interest in photography has become a big part of my life.

***

To see the world in a grain of sand,
And a heaven in a wild flower,
Hold infinity in the palm of your hand,
And eternity in an hour.

– William Blake

Afternoons Off

"Mourner, it calls you, – 'Come to my bosom,
Love wipes your tears all away,
And will lift the shade of gloom,
And for you make radiant room
Midst the glories of one endless day.'"
- Mary Baker Eddy

"I believe we're on earth to delight each other, make each other laugh, and to infuse one another with God's joy. Why not? What have we got better to do, for heaven's sake?"
– Burt Rosenberg

***

Without a doubt, the place where I've taken the most photos in my recent collection has been the boardwalk and connecting path that runs along the bay in Bellingham, 20 minutes to the north of my home. The boardwalk has provided me with new friendships, and a place of great peace and joy.

The Year of Insanity was a milestone for me – it had caused changes in the way I viewed the world, and I realized I was going to need to make some changes in my life to coincide with that new view. My priorities had shifted, and I'd come to the realization that I needed to make an effort to bring more balance to my life. I asked my employer if I could work half-time for a year and have the afternoons off. Much to my great joy, my employer granted my request.

***

That first afternoon off I walked around with a silly, giddy grin on my face. I felt like a little kid who's managed to grab the last cookie out of the cookie jar.

It was beautiful and sunny – not a cloud in the sky – as I parked my car in the Fairhaven district of Bellingham. I grabbed my little backpack-purse and started walking past the funky gift shops and ethnic restaurants of Fairhaven. I had such a feeling of freedom that first afternoon. I still couldn't believe I'd managed to pull off this half-time gig for myself.

My mom and dad had sent me a little money for my birthday and I used part of it to take myself out to lunch at one of my favorite Mexican restaurants.

While I was sitting there, two gentlemen came in and sat down at a table across the room. They were really interesting gents, and I started eavesdropping. One of them was talking about a man he'd met at an airport in Mexico who had escaped from some war in the Congo. After I paid my bill I went over to talk to them. I told them that I had been a History major in college, and that I'd overheard them talking about some man escaping from the Congo to Mexico, and just had to find out more. So these gentlemen pulled out a chair, and invited me to sit down, and proceeded to regale me with all kinds of great stories. The Congo story (which had happened during some uprising in 1962); and stories about WWII - one of these fellows had gotten a purple heart during WWII - had taken some German shrapnel when he'd been serving as a medic, and had gotten a free ride to college out of it - had graduated Suma Cum Laude from some university ("There were only two of us that year," he joked) and gone on to get a PhD in Romance Languages.

After my chat with them, I went for a walk down by the water. It was beautiful and sunny and warm and it felt like I was on a holiday. I felt kind of guilty - knowing that most people I knew were working or going to school - and here I was, strolling along the boardwalk in the sunshine. I had this big grin on my face, and as a couple of women about my age walked by me, I couldn't resist saying, "Isn't it great to have the afternoons off? I've never done this before!" And they both started laughing and agreed that having the afternoons off really rocked.

I was really conscious that when I came home from my "holiday" I needed to share the sunshine and cheer with Scott and the sons, who would be coming home tired and worn-down. So I came home, cleaned up the house, and put left-overs in the oven. When the sons came home, they actually noticed that the house was clean, and were thrilled to find dinner waiting for them. It was just a really satisfying feeling to be able to give that to them, and to not have to rush around, trying to get things done, all tired and cranky from work.

***

Taking afternoons off that year was one of the best possible things I could have done for myself, and for the people I love.

The Bellingham boardwalk became a place of spiritual uplift for me. I never went there but that I failed to be inspired by the beauty of Bellingham Bay, and the joyfulness of the people I met on my walks.

I made wonderful friendships on the boardwalk – among them, Lena and Mark, and the man with the twinkly eyes who liked to watch the water fowl with me. What was so freeing for me about these friendships was that there were no expectations built into them – none of these new friends expected anything from me, they were happy just to laugh and enjoy our brief moments together as we paused to chat on the boardwalk.

In his book *The Shack*, William P. Young writes, "If you and I are friends, there is an expectancy of being together, of laughing and talking... But what happens if I change that 'expectancy' to an 'expectation' – spoken or unspoken? Suddenly, law has entered into our relationship. You are now expected to perform in a way that meets my expectations... Responsibilities and expectations are the basis of guilt and shame and judgment, and they provide the essential framework that promotes performance as the basis for identity and value."

Humans, I think, have a tendency to judge and compare, contrast, and rank things. I've always thought of myself as a pretty non-judgmental person, on the whole – but I recently realized that I've had a tendency to judge my friendships with people – not the people involved in the friendships – but the friendships themselves. "This friendship is better than that one. This friendship is more important to me. This friendship isn't so important." And isn't that just a ridiculous way of looking at my relationships with others? There's no need to judge my friendships. They are what they are, and I need to just let myself enjoy them for what they are.

The friends I met on the boardwalk were friends without expectations of me or responsibility towards me. They weren't going to judge me or condemn me if I failed to meet certain 'expectations,' and I certainly wasn't going to judge or condemn them, either.

It was great.

And I very much enjoyed (and still enjoy!) my friendships with The People of the Boardwalk.

***

Now that I had the time to, literally, "stop and smell the roses" – I began to look at it as a sort of joyful duty to God to do just that. An artist needs someone to appreciate her art. As I watched people rushing around – trying to get from one place to the next as quickly as they could, running to increase their heart rate, or running to get to their next appointment - I began to feel that God's "art" wasn't being seen or appreciated as it should, and I began to think of it as a sort of mission to slow down and walk through God's gallery with the deliberate and thoughtful appreciation for Her expression that the awe-inspiring beauty around me warranted.

From my journal –

The last couple times I've come to the boardwalk I've felt these incredible moments of peace and contentment and well-being. I feel God speaking to me in the laughter and the sparkling waves and the blossoms dancing in the wind – and I feel what He's sharing and giving to me is special and unique to me alone – like He's reaching me in the exact way I need to be reached – and I guess that comes from my own unique perceptions and response to what I'm seeing. God's talking like this to me all the time – there's this constant good going on – but I don't always see it or feel it, because I let myself get distracted by stuff that's not real or valuable or important. Right here, where I might see fear and anger and hate – in this exact same place and space, there's another universe filled with incredible good – and I have a choice of which one I want to live in, and which one I want to see as 'real.'

As I sat in the sun on the bench on the knoll yesterday, looking out at the bay, all the ego-stuff and politicking just disappeared, and had no importance to me at all. And I was filled with such a feeling of good will – I just sent my thoughts out to everyone – hoping they'd feel the peace I felt. "Happiness is spiritual, born of Truth and Love. It is unselfish; therefore it cannot exist alone, but requires all mankind to share it," Mary Baker Eddy says. When I'm feeling strong and happy I want to shine that feeling on others – because I know there'll be times when I'll need that from them, too.

Yesterday I knew and felt God's love for me – and what others' thought about me just was not a concern. I felt like God was proud of me, and that was all that mattered.

Walked about six miles today – along the boardwalk and into downtown Bellingham. I was surrounded by Spring on my walk – by greenery and blossoms – and I realized that Nature and I had made it through the winter together. Nature, as the expression of God, had never been panicked about winter – it just calmly prepared for summer, never doubting it'd make it. Steady and calm. Glad I got to experience all the seasons again during my year of afternoons off. We've come full circle, Nature and me.

Nature

> *"For ye shall go out with joy, and be led forth with peace: the mountains and the hills shall break forth before you into singing, and all the trees of the field shall clap their hands."*
> *– Isaiah 55:12*

> *"Nature voices natural, spiritual law and divine Love, but human belief misinterprets nature. Arctic regions, sunny tropics, giant hills, winged winds, mighty billows, verdant vales, festive flowers, and glorious heavens, - all point to Mind, the spiritual intelligence they reflect. The floral apostles are hieroglyphs of Deity. Suns and planets teach grand lessons. The stars make night beautiful, and the leaflet turns naturally towards the light."*
> *- Mary Baker Eddy*

> *"The best remedy for those who are afraid, lonely or unhappy is to go outside, somewhere where they can be quiet, alone with the heavens, nature and God. Because only then does one feel that all is as it should be."*
> *- Anne Frank*

***

Nature has been a huge solace and comfort to me during my Middle Book. When I'm outside, amongst trees and birds, or standing on a beach looking towards the sea, I feel connected to something beyond myself. It's impossible for me to feel lonely, or depressed, or friendless, when I'm immersed in the life of creation.

***

October 31st: The walkways are covered in gold right now, and gold drops from the trees around us. The air is filled with that musty, dying-leaf, pungent apple cider smell of autumn. And the wind! Great gusts of it blowing against the house, slashing rain against the windows. And I sit inside in the evenings with a fire in the woodstove and a cup of tea at my elbow and a good book. Bliss.

November 14th: We had a marvelous hike! There were patches of fog in the trees - which was really dramatic and cool - made the bare branches and trunks stand out against the white - and here and there were splashes of gold and yellow and orange where the last of the leaves still clung to their branches. Beautiful!

January 24th: It's been cold and clear and beautiful here! Picture it: To the east, a full moon rising over snow-covered hills, trumpeter swans glowing white in the fields. Four of them fly directly overhead, honking. Eagles sitting in the trees waiting for prey. To the west, the sun sets orangey-pink on the Puget Sound, reflecting on the water. Brilliant colors! And the days are getting longer! And little buds are popping out on the trees and birds are singing...

May 8th : Saw a coyote on the way to work yesterday. It was just sitting in a field, sort of looking around in a really nonchalant way. When I stopped the car, he got up and looked like he was ready to take flight. I fumbled around in my bag and finally managed to pull out my camera – got a picture just before he scampered off.
Man, it was magic – there's something really cool about seeing a wild coyote – it's like making contact with a creature from another world, you know?

May 9th: We had an absolutely lovely day today - soft and gentle - apple blossoms, tulips, the smell of the alders opening themselves up to the sunshine. No coyotes today, but the birds were busy and singing...

May 19th: When I went on my walk yesterday I felt like God wanted to play – like She was excited and was enjoying Her creation and just wanted to shower me with Her gifts, to celebrate with me and watch my delight – like She was happy I was in Her presence and excited to show-off Her creation with me. The birds are singing, blossoms are bursting out all around me, and lambs are bouncing around in the fields.
And I feel like I have risen above a really crippling sense of guilt. I feel free.

May 26: There's this great line from *Jurassic Park*: by Michael Crichton: "Life will find a way." That's what Spring feels like to me – like Life is just bursting out all around me, breaking through the winter, clothing the trees with new leaves, unfolding in the blossoms – and bursting out of me, too. There is renewal here. Nothing can stop it. Life is finding its way.
When I hear the birds singing, it feels like God is speaking to me. I feel like all of creation is celebrating Spring, and I've been invited to a really cool party…

June 11th: You know - I've always felt really connected to Nature - but lately I've been experiencing something kind of ... well, "transcendental" might be the word. I've made a conscious effort to shut out all the dialogue that's continually going on in my head and just tune in to the world outside me, and all its sounds - the birds singing, the whooshing sound the leaves on the trees make, traffic in the distance. And I'm seeing things maybe I never noticed before - individual petals on flowers, the flickering of individual leaves, the changes from one moment to the next. It's just amazing the way everything around me is moving in harmony, dancing to some universal rhythm - and everything is where it should be, moving where it should move, filling its own niche, serving its own purpose...

June 21st: Went on a hike with Teresa a couple of weeks ago and this really cool thing happened: An owl flew down and landed on a tree branch right in front of us. Pretty soon another owl joined the first one. The two of them just sat there on that branch, blinking at us - totally unafraid. I was able to get out my camera and take pictures of them. It was like magic - I've rarely had the chance to see one owl in the daylight, let alone TWO! I think they must have been youngsters - they were kind of fluffy-looking, like they still had some downy feathers - and they were innocently unafraid of us.
Anyway, that kind of experience always makes me feel blest - like Creation is giving me a gift.

June 24th: It was so amazing out tonight. I love the way everything smells when the sun sets and the air gets cool and kind of damp - everything smells more keen and clear, you know? I could smell the hay fields - I love the smell of freshly-mowed hay - and the flowers, and the sappy smell of the fir trees. The moon was shining through a really thin veil of clouds, and the stars were peeking out and winking at me. And I could hear the bats sending out their radar. I really like that sound...

July 3rd: I had a sort of spiritual musical moment today. I was getting ready to balance my checkbook and was not looking forward to it, and felt the need to get myself inspired before I plunged into the world of numbers and money. So I put on U2's *Joshua Tree* - there's something about that album that always sort of uplifts me. And just as the music started going, a heavy rain started pouring from the heavens - but it was like the rain was celebrating with me, rather than trying to attack me, you know? - and it seemed to me it was pounding into the ground in the rhythm of the song, and it was like we were dancing together to the beat. I know. I am so weird. But, trust me, it was a really cool moment!

July 8th: Went to the ocean last weekend with the family. I came upon this rock wall that looked like a rainbow of sea creatures - turquoise-colored anemones, orange and red starfish, purply-blue mussels - it was so beautiful! Like a mosaic from Nature...

July 15th: The moon was glowing, almost full, above the wheat field. It was that time of evening - just after the sun sets, when the light has a soft golden quality to it, and the sky has layers of blue and yellow and pink. Everything is settled and quiet, and the air has that freshness to it that comes as everything cools off for the day. There was the smell of honeysuckle and roses. A couple of bats flew overhead, darting and dodging, chasing after the mosquitoes.

I do love summer evenings.

***

Okay, so I had this epiphany the other morning. And it's going to sound really trite – because I think it's something that a lot of people recognize on some level and it's nothing new I'm going to say, but... anyway...

You know how when you look up at the stars at night you get a feeling that you're part of something really amazing and awesome? And for me, it feels like I'm part of some big purpose, too.

So the other day I'm at a beach on the Puget Sound, and I have it entirely to myself, and as I look out at the water, and watch the little sea creatures in the tidal pool next to me, I get that same feeling – that I'm part of something awesome, and that I'm part of some universal purpose. And it came to me that the purpose of everything, the purpose of the universe, is to love. And everything else – the mistakes we make, and the struggles we have – if those things lead us to understand love better, and lead us to love more – then that's all that matters, really.

And right after my epiphany, this family came around the corner, and their dog came barreling straight for me and leaped on me and licked my face and just showered his slobbery love on me... it was great!

***

"Presence is needed to become aware of the beauty, the majesty, the sacredness of nature... You have to put down for a moment your personal baggage of problems, of past and future, as well as your knowledge; otherwise, you will see but not see, hear but not hear. Your total presence is required."
- Ekhart Tolle

"Hearing-beyond"

"Whatever inspires with wisdom, Truth, or Love – be it song, sermon, or Science – blesses the human family with crumbs of comfort from Christ's table, feeding the hungry and giving living waters to the thirsty." – Mary Baker Eddy

"...David and all Israel played music before God with all their might, with singing, on harps, on stringed instruments, on tambourines, on cymbals, and with trumpets."
– I *Chronicles* 13: 8

"Music in the soul can be heard by the universe". – Lao Tzu

***

One of my all-time favorite books is a story authored by Lois Lowery called *The Giver*. The book was written for middle schoolers, but I think it has a wonderful message for adults, too. In this story one boy, Jonas, is chosen to become *The Receiver* – the person who holds all the memories of his community, so that the rest of the people in his community don't need to be burdened by them. One of the indicators that he's right for this position is an ability for *seeing-beyond* – which we eventually learn means that he can see colors, when everyone else in his community can only see in black-and-white. The old Receiver – now known as The Giver - has a special talent, too, it turns out. In the book, The Giver tells Jonas: "When I was just a boy, younger than you, it began to come to me. But it wasn't the seeing-beyond for me. It was different. For me, it was *hearing*-beyond." Jonas asks him what he heard, and The Giver answers: "I began to hear something truly remarkable, and it is called music."

I love that! I think it's really profound of Lois Lowery to compare music with color. Harmony, melody, and lyrics can inspire and stir me in the same way that a rainbow, or autumn leaves, or a sunset over the ocean does. There are certain songs that, when performed well, can bring spontaneous tears to my eyes, and a smile to my face, and fill me with joy.

***

> *"I have a dream, a song to sing*
> *To help me cope with anything*
> *If you see the wonder of a fairy tale*
> *You can take the future even if you fail*
> *I believe in angels*
> *Something good in everything I see*
> *I believe in angels*
> *When I know the time is right for me*
> *I'll cross the stream - I have a dream."- ABBA*

When I first heard about the movie, *Mamma Mia*, I wasn't terribly interested in it. I'd never been a really big ABBA fan, and I couldn't see myself sitting through two hours of their music. But Kathi had mentioned that she was hoping to see it. And, because I was learning that what she liked, I usually ended up liking, too, I decided to give it a go.

***

The movie started with an ethereal setting. - stars and water and a beautiful young girl singing, "I have a dream, a song to sing, to help me cope with anything." Hope. There was hope in those lyrics.

As the movie unfolded, I found myself getting pulled in. When Meryl Streep sang the title song it called to the man-loving romantic in me; when her two friends sang *Chicaquita* to her, I found myself choking back a sob, wishing I had those two friends to tell me that I wasn't a bad person, and that I was worth comforting; and when Meryl was feeling shamed and guilty about her past indiscretions, and her friends put it all in perspective for her, and told her to "Screw 'em if they can't take a joke!" I wanted to applaud. And then there was *Dancing Queen* – that song spoke to every woman in that theater, both young and old, who'd ever known the heady joy of feeling attractive and wanted, and I wanted to get out of my seat and join Meryl and her friends in their sassy celebration of fun and freedom. When Pierce and Meryl sang *SOS*, I thought of my relationship to my husband – somewhere along the way we'd started taking each other for granted and lost something – and *SOS* reminded me of the something we'd lost.

And the tears streamed down my face when Meryl sang, *Slipping Through My Fingers* – the bittersweet song of a mother who's about to watch her grown child leave home for a new life: "Sleep in our eyes/ Her and me at the breakfast table/ Barely awake/ I let precious time go by/ Then when she's gone/ There's that odd melancholy feeling/ And a sense of guilt/ I can't deny/ What happened to the wonderful adventures/ The places I had planned for us to go/ Well some of that we did/ But most we didn't/ And why I just don't know."

This movie was about me.

I walked out of that theater feeling weirdly cleansed - baptized in joy, and atoned in sass.

I had to share what I'd just experienced with someone else. I thought of my friend, Teresa. I knew she would get that movie. Teresa shares the same intensity for living and life that I do, and I knew she would understand it in the same way I did – that she'd realize that there was more to *Mamma Mia* than light-hearted music with a good beat. As I sat next to Teresa in the theater, I was not disappointed – tears glistened in her eyes, a grin appeared on her face, she sniffled as Streep sang, "Slipping Through My Fingers" and laughed out loud when Meryl Streep said, "I haven't slept with THOUSANDS of men."

Next I took Scott to see it. I was really hoping he'd like it, and was so happy when he told me he did. His favorite part of the movie? When Pierce Brosnan and Meryl Streep sang *SOS*. Scott got it.

And then came ABBA's *When All Is Said and Done*:

"Here's to us, one more toast and then we'll pay the bill
Deep inside both of us can feel the autumn chill
Birds of passage, you and me, we fly instinctively
When the summer's over and the dark clouds hide the sun
Neither you nor I'm to blame when all is said and done
In our lives we have walked some strange and lonely treks
Slightly worn but dignified and not too old for sex
Standin' calmly at the crossroads, no desire to run
There's no hurry any more when all is said and done"

That song was an affirmation that everything would be alright for us, in the end.

***

As I began to spread the word about *Mamma Mia*, I began to see a pattern in the types of people who enjoyed it. My mom and dad loved that movie and ended up seeing it probably four or five times. Scott's mom and sister enjoyed it, too. My brother liked it. Kathi saw it and loved it, and when I sent a *Mamma Mia* DVD to Kathi and Jamie for Christmas, I was told that even Jamie (who is notorious for his movie-pickiness and whose favorite movie is *A Clockwork Orange*) liked it. (!)

On the other hand, another friend – one who sometimes has an unfortunate tendency to be a little judgmental and a bit rigid – saw it with me and I could feel her reining her joy in as she watched it. At the end she pronounced it "cute." I suppose *Mamma Mia* is "cute" – but that wouldn't be the one word I'd use to sum it up.

Mamma Mia celebrated the joy of living and loving, without condemnation or judgment. It was shameless. And I desperately needed "shameless" just then.

***

I recently had a wonderful drive with Alison Krauss. Well, okay, Alison Krauss wasn't actually in the car with me. But her voice was. And it was lovely.

I was driving home, after a visit with my parents, and just as I got to Seattle big, fluffy snowflakes started floating down around me. It was like being inside one of those glass bubbles that has "snow" trapped inside it. It was dark, and the snow made it even more difficult to see, but I was suddenly filled with such a sense of peace and joy, that driving felt more like a celebration than a hazard. I'd put an Alison Krauss CD in my car's CD-player, and, as the snow started falling, her delightful riff leading into the Beatles *I Will* filled my car with a playfulness and a joy that was almost tangible. I realized that the cars around me were moving in complete harmony with me and with the song – it was like we were all doing a happy dance together – perfectly-timed and choreographed.

"Who knows how long I've loved you? You know I love you still..." I'd always thought those words and that song were romantic – it was a song I'd sung at least once at a wedding. But now I found those words and that song taking on a different meaning for me. My mom's sweet, smiling face came into focus in my thoughts and I held her there for a moment – just completely filled with the joy of the love we share for each other. Then my Dad came through my thoughts, and I mentally hugged him; then my husband, my sons, my co-workers, my bosses, my neighbors, my friends – even those with whom I'd had conflict – one-by-one passed through my thoughts. And as each new face appeared I mentally wrapped love and joy around my thoughts of that person. The playful, irrepressible joy of that song, and Krauss's performance of it, simply could not be overthrown or trampled down. Anger and frustration had no choice but to melt away before the happy onslaught of banjos and love.

It was a transforming experience for me, and when the snow finally stopped falling and the song had ended, I felt like I'd just been privileged to be a part of something magical and wondrous. The feeling of joy still lingers.

Later I thought some more about the song and its words:

> *"Who knows how long I've loved you*
> *You know I love you still*
> *Will I wait a lonely lifetime?*
> *If you want me to, I will.*
> *I love you forever and forever*
> *Love you with all my heart*
> *Love you whenever we're together*
> *Love you when we're apart.*
> *And when at last I find you*
> *Your song will fill the air*
> *Sing it loud so I can hear you*
> *Make it easy to be near you*

For the things you do, endear you to me
Oh, you know I will, I will"

And it occurred to me that God, Love itself, could sing those words to you and me. How long has God loved us? Forever and ever and for always. She loves us when we're near Her in our thoughts, and She loves us when we're not. She loves us when we know Her, and She loves us when we don't. And we are dear and precious to Her. "I will, I will," are our Father-Mother God's words and promise to us. Unconditional, unfailing love is ours to give, and ours to receive.

***

One of my favorite songs of all-time is George Harrison's *Here Comes the Sun*. I remember hearing that song come on the radio one day, as I was nearing the end of the winter of my depression – and I instantly found myself with a big grin on my face.

What a celebration of survival! What a celebration of life!

"Little darling
The smiles returning to the faces
Little darling
It seems like years since it's been here
Here comes the sun
Here comes the sun, and I say
It's all right
Little darling
I feel that ice is slowly melting
Little darling
It seems like years since it's been clear
Here comes the sun
Here comes the sun, and I say
It's all right..."

How can a person hear that song and *not* feel inspired and joyful and ready to celebrate life?!
***

"Mental melodies and strains of sweetest music supersede conscious sound. Music is the rhythm of head and heart." – Mary Baker Eddy

In This Moment

"Take therefore no thought for the morrow: for the morrow shall take thought for the things of itself..." – Matthew 6: 34

"You can always cope with the present moment, but you cannot cope with something that is only a mind projection – you cannot cope with the future." – Eckhart Tolle

"The time to be happy is now; the place to be happy is here." – Robert Ingersoll

***

The power of a moment
Each one ripe with possibilities
Each one bringing the opportunity
of the first meeting of a new friend,
a new insight, a cessation
of pain, a sweet kiss, a lark's trill,
a glimmer of light on water,
a precious memory,
a healing.
For this moment, whole with life,
you are safe, alive, breathing, moving,
supplied with all you need.
Right now you are perfect.
Right now you can claim everything good for yourself.
In this moment, right now, you are beautiful,
satisfied, fearless, loved, loving,
witness to perfection, beauty, and good.
In this moment
catch the beauty of Now

Travels with the Madcap Christian Scientist

"Certainly, travel is more than the seeing of sights; it is a change that goes on, deep and permanent, in the ideas of living." – Miriam Beard

"And so by the fifteenth century, on October 8, the Europeans were looking for a new place to try to get to, and they came up with a new concept: the West." – Dave Barry

"And remember, no matter where you go, there you are." – Confucius

***

I've always enjoyed traveling – meeting new people and exploring new places, and spending time together with my loved ones, away from the busy-ness of our everyday life. There were a couple of trips after the Year of Insanity that were significant to me, and I'd like to share them with you.

***

Our trip to Nova Scotia was a Big Deal. I'd wanted to visit that part of the world for a long time – I'd heard from others who'd been there about the rugged, natural beauty of the coastline and forests, the brightly-hued homes and shops, and the friendliness of the people. And after I met Jamie and Kathi on the internet, I had a real yearning to meet them in the person, too. So, on one of our trips back to the east coast to visit Scott's family, we set aside a weekend to spend time with Jamie and Kathi in Nova Scotia.

We reserved a place on the double-hulled hydro-ferry that was running from Portland, Maine to Yarmouth, Nova Scotia, thinking this might be the fastest way to get from where we were to where we wanted to go. (This ferry is no longer in service.)

We left Scott's folks' house in upstate New York in the middle of the night and drove up to Portland, arriving there at five or so in the morning. There weren't many people about when we arrived in Portland – the sun hadn't yet risen, and most of the businesses wouldn't open for several hours. But we found a great little diner next to the ferry terminal – Becky's Diner – and settled in for one of the best breakfasts I have ever eaten – I no longer remember the specifics, but I remember devouring a cheesy omelet and having a hot chocolate in a solid old-fashioned mug with *Becky's Diner* emblazoned on it (we ended up buying a couple of those mugs, and every time I get them out I think of Portland, Maine, Becky's Diner, and our friends in Nova Scotia).

I am not going to spend a lot of time talking about the ferry ride. There's a reason for this. Most of the passengers that day got seasick. My youngest son, Xander, and I were among them. Let's just say that the wonderful breakfast I'd eaten at Becky's Diner did not stay in me very long. Let me also say that, as Scott moved amongst the afflicted offering water and sick bags, and Andrew slept his way through the rocking seas – the whole experience was a bonding one for Xander and me, huddled down together on the outside deck. I suppose I probably sang some hymns from the *Christian Science Hymnal*, and probably recited some passages from *Science and Health* that I always find helpful to me – but honestly, I don't remember much about the whole experience anymore, except the camaraderie Xander and I felt in our time of mutual suffering.

When we finally arrived, once again, on land, I asked Scotty to pull over at a restroom so that I could make an attempt to clean myself up and change clothes. The prospect of meeting Kathi and Jamie for the first time, with vestiges of puke on my person, was not one that appealed to me.

On the way to their home, we drove by beautiful scenery – lots of lakes and ponds, wetlands and forests, and green everywhere, and as I snapped pictures from the car window, I was filled with a weird mix of eager anticipation, and a sort of nervous apprehension. What if…? What if when they saw me they took an instant dislike to me for some reason? What if I was a disappointment to them? What if they ended up being not at all as they'd presented themselves to me, and I ended up putting my family in danger? Would they like me? Would my family like them?

And then we were turning up their street, and there was their home! Kathi had sent me pictures of it – brightly-colored and cheerful-looking – and I recognized it instantly!

There was a tallish, lanky, pony-tailed man at the end of the driveway, walking around a boat there, like he was inspecting it. This had to be Jamie… "Jamie?" I asked, getting out of the car and walking up to him. It was totally surreal - like meeting in person a favorite character from a well-loved novel. Without thought, I reached up to give him a hug, and he hugged me back, then I introduced him to Scott and the sons, and soon I was hugging Kathi, and then I was in her kitchen, watching her slice peppers, and watching her put things in the oven and take wonderful-smelling things out of the oven, and then we were all sitting together at the table on their back porch, eating one of the best meals I have ever eaten anywhere in my life – did I mention Kathi is a gourmet chef? – and I know this was a run-on sentence, but only a run-on sentence can convey what it all felt like for me.

They were exactly who I'd imagined them to be.

Jamie's wry and witty observations about life made me laugh out loud – as he'd always managed to do on the religion forum. And Kathi's welcoming warmth and generosity made us feel right at home. And their house was amazing! – there were joyful, vibrant colors on every wall, furniture that looked like it came from a fairy tale, and books filling every nook and cranny. And I finally met their new kitty, Chloe, and their beagle, Deiter, and I even caught a glimpse of their elusive old male cat, Ed.

Kathi and Jamie's home was my kind of home.

The next day Jamie and Kathi took us to Green Bay for a picnic and a walk along the ocean.

It was a spectacular day in every way.

We walked along the beach for awhile, exploring the tide pools and watching the waves tumble across the rocks – Jamie plucked a couple of wild rose blossoms and tucked them behind Kathi's ear and mine – and he and Scott talked about carpentering, while the sons climbed boulders and gazed out at the Atlantic, and Jamie and Kathi's beagle, Deiter, ran circles around us, sniffing the crevices and holes between the rocks. When it was time to eat, we discovered that Kathi's idea of a "picnic" was not your basic cheese sandwich and potato chips. Jamie had packed in four big bowls full of elaborate dishes Kathi had created that included ingredients of shrimp, mushrooms, and baby potatoes. It was the kind of feast you'd expect to find in a cordon bleu restaurant. And here we were, nestled on the boulders along Green Bay, with the Atlantic Ocean to the east, and a lush green woodland to the west, eating like royalty. After our picnic, Kathi and I walked on a trail along the beach to a spot where the waterfront's owner had provided a camera for people to take a picture of themselves. That was cool. Kathi and I brought our heads together and took a self-portrait for the camera's owner and then retraced our steps back to the cars.

Jamie and Kathi's beagle, Deiter, had been following us, and when we were about half-way back, we realized she was no longer with us. This was concerning.

By this time the sun was setting, and the moon was rising above Green Bay. It was a lovely evening, but it was getting dark, and we were all worried about Deiter. Jamie left their phone number with some people who lived on the beach, in case someone found Deiter, and we left Green Bay without her.

As it says in *The Bible,* "there is nothing lost that shall not be found" and, happily, the next day, when we arrived back at Kathi and Jamie's for our last morning with them, Deiter had been found and was back in the bosom of her family, once again.

Our last morning there we drove with Jamie and Kathi into Lunenberg to walk through a shop where a room had been set aside for Kathi's colorful wood carvings. Her art is joyful and fun, and it put a grin on my face to walk into an entire room with its walls covered by her whimsical, cheery carvings of mermaids, fish, and stars.

We had a last farewell meal together at an Italian restaurant in town. It was really hard to say good-bye to my new friends. But I was so grateful to have finally been able to meet them in the person, and so grateful to find that they were as wonderful face-to-face as they were on my computer. I was really glad, too, that Scott and the sons had enjoyed Jamie and Kathi as much as I did. The sons were hugely impressed by Kathi's cooking – "She even makes vegetables taste good!" they said, in awe.

On our return to the United States, we took a different route, crossing the Bay of Fundy to New Brunswick. That ferry ride was much more comfortable than the ferry ride from Portland to Yarmouth, and Scott and I stood together on the deck of the boat most of the way, scanning the vast horizon of the bay, and breathing in the brisk, salty air. I am happy to report that neither Xander nor I lost our cookies on the return trip.

***

During the Year of Insanity, when Andrew had accompanied me on the trip to the Oregon coast, Xander had mentioned that this was something he'd like to do with me someday, too.

I guess I didn't really expect Alexander to still want to take a trip with me, once he reached 16. It still surprised me that Andrew had been willing to go with me on a vacation when he was a teenager. But when Xander turned 16, I asked him, anyway – hoping he'd still want to go with me, but expecting him to say *nah*. Much to my delighted surprised, Xander said that he would, indeed, like to go with me to Lincoln City, on the Oregon coast.

The day before we left, I kept going through the checklist with Xander. "Did you pack your swimsuit? Did you pack a pair of long pants? A pair of shorts? A sweatshirt? Toothbrush? Sneakers? Sandals?" I'd ask. And then half an hour later, I'd go through the routine with him again: "Swimsuit? Jeans? Shorts? Sweatshirt? Toothbrush? Sneakers? Sandals?" Xander was very patient with me, and kept assuring me that he was, indeed, packed and ready to go.

The moment finally arrived when it was time to leave. We loaded our belongings into the car, took one final look at our home, and then began our seven-hour journey to Lincoln City, Oregon.

We had a wonderful drive down – stopped at my favorite restaurant in Olympia for pizza on the way, and ran into no major traffic jams or anything.

Before long we were at the motel, unloading the car.

And this is when I realized that none of the stuff *I'd* packed was in there – my backpack full of clothes, my laptop, my toothbrush and other sundries – none of it was in the car! I had a moment when I panicked – wondered if somehow someone had managed to steal it all when we'd been parked at the restaurant, or at a rest stop maybe. I called home and Scott answered the phone. He informed me (and I'm pretty sure there was some amusement in his voice) that everything I'd packed was still sitting by the front door. He and Andrew had, apparently, not noticed this until 40 minutes before, or they would have called me.

It was a great relief to know my things hadn't been stolen – and once I realized everything was safe – there was this sense of freedom about it all. I wasn't going to be encumbered by a lot of things I didn't really need.

It was all a little humbling for me, too. Note that Xander had not been the one to leave everything behind in Bow. He had his "swimsuit, jeans, shorts, sweatshirt, and toothbrush" and all the things that he'd felt were essential for him on this trip - while I... ahem... did not.

I told Xander that I was depending on him to take care of his senile old mom. He started laughing (and man! I discovered on this trip that Alexander Terrell has a really wonderful sense of humor about life – he has this great bubbly laughter) and said, "Senile? No. Crazy? Probably." And he really did take care of me on this trip – he was really easy-going about all our adventures and misadventures and just sort of went with it all.

We had some great conversations about life – talked about friendships and family and history (he's a great history buff) and religion and God and work and scientific discoveries and what's important to each of us.

At some point Andrew texted Xander with this cryptic message: "Guess what Paul did today?" (Paul is Xander's fish.) So Xander texted back to find out what his fish had done, and Andrew wrote back: "Nothing. He's a fish."

Then Andrew let Alexander know that this big video chain was closing and that he and Scott had gotten some really great deals on DVDs. Xander got all excited about this, and wanted to get back home right away so he could buy all kinds of DVDs. I let him know that we wouldn't be getting back until late on the following Tuesday, and he got a little bummed, I think – but he just sort of let go of it.

We had a great time at the beach – looked for agates, flew a kite, explored the tide pools and found a clump of colorful starfish latched onto the rocks. And I somehow managed to survive for three days without my laptop or the internet. It was fantastic.

And here's a really cool thing: On our way home, as we were passing through a little Oregon seaside town, I looked over to a small group of box stores and saw one of the video stores of the chain that was closing! Xander got all excited. I pulled over, and we went into the store, and he ended up finding all the movies he'd been hoping to buy, for a very good price.

On the way home, I made the mistake of taking a kind of obscure highway from Astoria, Oregon – I thought it'd be a shortcut to the freeway, but no – this road was, like, 50 miles of serpentining, over-hill-and-dale, curving road. It was like hell. Xander and I started laughing about that – that maybe we were *in* hell – that this is what it would look like – going on forever with no end in sight. I was starting to run low on gas by this time, too – and there were absolutely no gas stations, anywhere. I finally turned into a farm – I was starting to panic and had to get some idea of where we were. The farm had a honeysuckle bush, a calico cat, and windchimes – and I figured anyone with a honeysuckle bush, a calico cat, and windschimes couldn't be too scary. I knocked on the door, and a man who was on his cellphone looked up with a surprised look on his face.

He came outside and joined me on his deck and reassured me I had enough gas to make it to the next gas station, and gave me directions to the freeway. He was very cool. He said he'd been about to take a nap when the phone rang, and then someone knocked on his door – and no one ever knocks on his door! It had been a very exciting day for him, he told me.

Xander and I did, of course, manage to make it to a gas station, and safely home.

It remains one of the best road trips I have ever taken.

The Christmas Cat

"Who would believe such pleasure from a wee ball o' fur?" - Irish Saying

"If there were to be a universal sound depicting peace, I would surely vote for the purr."
– Barbara L. Diamond

***

In *Blessings: Adventures of a Madcap Christian Scientist* I tell the story of our Christmas Dog – a dog I'd found on Christmas Eve who had been shot in the head. The Christmas Dog survived the shooting, and ended up becoming a much-loved member of our family, until her death more than a decade later.

Now, in this book, I have the pleasure of telling you about the Christmas *cat*.

Just before Christmas, Alexander came home from his walk with our dog, Sam, to tell me that they'd found a bloodied little calico cat on the side of the road. I grabbed a towel and followed Xander to the kitty. She was curled up on the side of the road, not moving much – except for one twitchy ear. She hissed defensively when I reached down to hold her, but I wrapped her up in the towel so she couldn't scratch and held her close to me. I told the son to get my car keys and purse and meet me at the car, and I slowly carried the kitty back to our house.

Once I was holding her, she stopped hissing and fidgeting, and when I sat down in the car with her, she relaxed against me, laid her head on my arm and began to purr as I petted her head and ears. As the son drove us to the vet's I sang the song I'd once sung, years ago, to the Christmas Dog.

"Everlasting arms of Love, are beneath, around, above…" (words by John R. MacDuff) and the kitty looked up at me with the same look of trust and love that the Christmas Dog had once shown me.

I'll be honest, the picture was not pretty. She looked to have been hit in the head by a car. Her jaw was out of alignment, and her eyes were filling up with blood. In my thoughts, I tried to establish who this little kitty was, as an expression of God – tried to establish her in my thoughts as God's perfect idea, held whole, complete, and untouched by accident, in the consciousness of Love. What gave me some courage and confidence about the whole situation was the kitty herself – she seemed calm, totally unaware that she looked a mess, and completely content just resting on my lap, wrapped up in the towel. She was…well…she was very matter-of-fact about it all, to tell you the truth – like nothing out of the ordinary had just happened to her.

When we got to the vet's I carried her inside (she was still purring), and the dear receptionist and assistant there immediately, but gently, removed the cat from my arms and whisked her away to a backroom. Before I left her there, they told me that a microchip had been found on her and that they'd try to contact the owners. I told them that if they couldn't find the owners, I'd be willing to take responsibility for the kitty. (In the short drive to the vet's she'd already managed to capture my heart.)

The next morning I called the vet's to get an update, and was relieved to learn that the kitty was still alive, was actually doing "pretty good," and was still purring. The owner had come in and decisions were being made as to how to proceed regarding the kitty's jaw, which had been shattered.

A couple of days later, on our way to church, we noticed our next-door neighbors had a sign in their front yard that read "slow down" and we wondered if there might be some connection between that sign and the kitty-cat we'd found near their house two days before. That night I knocked on their door and found that they were, indeed, the owners of that kitty. They brought me in to look at her. She was snugly ensconced in a kitty carrier, half-dozing, and looking much better than she did when I first met her. The neighbors were happy to learn that I'd been the person the doctor had referred to as "The Good Samaritan." "Mystery solved!" said Robert with a grin - and *I* was happy to learn that my neighbors were the owners of that dear kitty – I knew she was in a good home if she was living with them.

Several months have gone by since we discovered the calico kitty on the side of the road. A few days ago I looked out onto our back deck and saw a calico cat out there, exploring it. It took me a moment to realize the cat was the cat we'd brought to the vet in December! It made me so happy to see her looking fit and healthy. And then, yesterday, she came up to me while I was in the garden, and let me pick her up and cuddle her. It was wonderful to hear her purr again.

I'm really grateful that Xander and I got to have a part in her rescue.

Never Separated from Love

"In Science, individual good derived from God, the infinite All-in-all, may flow from the departed to mortals..."
– Mary Baker Eddy

"For I am persuaded, that neither death, nor life, nor angels, nor principalities, nor powers, nor things present, nor things to come, Nor height, nor depth, nor any other creature, shall be able to separate us from the love of God, which is in Christ Jesus our Lord."
- Romans 8: 38-39

"Celebrate me, for I lived and loved and learned, and you were all part of my celebration of life."
– Melinda Walsh

***

I sat on Thom Bishop's bench again recently. Closed my eyes and listened to the sounds around me – bicycle bells, seagulls, children laughing – sounds that I've come to associate with The Bench. I breathed in the briny air, settled into the warmth of the sunshine, and thought back to the person I was when I first sat on the bench, and the person I'd become since then.

I'd discovered Thom's bench on my daily afternoon walks during the year I worked half-days. The bench faces into the afternoon sun, sitting on a small rise above the boardwalk that skirts Bellingham Bay. As soon as I saw it, I recognized it as a perfect place for peaceful meditation, and left the boardwalk to check it out. The words and dates on the plaque in front of the bench captured my attention: "Thom Bishop. Born January 24, 1955. Died July 31, 1974. Grounded before he could soar. Celebrate me, for I lived and loved and learned, and you were all part of my celebration of life. – Melinda Walsh." Thom had been born a year and half before me, and had died shortly after I graduated from high school - I felt a kinship to him, and I had all kinds of questions about Thom. I wondered about the manner of his death, wondered about his life, wondered what he'd looked like.

I finally googled him and was able to find an interview with a woman who'd been a friend of Thom's in high school (Kamalla, *The Sixties at WWU*, August 2007, **http://fairhaven.tribe.net/m/thread/8e1a07ee-e813-45cd-be9d-7d4fd4c3c711**). She said he'd looked like an "elf" and that he'd come from a family of peace activists. She described how Thom had helped young men escape to Canada by throwing Frisbees over the border at the Peace Park in Blaine, Washington, giving draft escapees chasing the Frisbee the means of running across the border to freedom.

This glimmer into Thom's life fascinated me. I began to see him as a brave young hero, a life-saver, an adventurous radical, and my curiosity about him grew.

Because he died so young, I speculated that he'd probably been killed in an accident – and a car accident seemed the most likely. Finally, after months of speculation, my curiosity needed to be sated. And so, walking the length of the boardwalk to the downtown area of Bellingham, I visited the *Bellingham Herald* office – I thought the newspaper might have a story about Thom's death in its archives. I was told by the receptionist that Thom had died too long ago for the Herald to have the story, but she suggested I visit the Bellingham Public Library and look through the microfiche records there.

I drove to the library the next day – filled with an excited anticipation about what I might learn about Thom. Because Thom had died on the last day in July, I was given microfiche for both July and August. I started with July, reeling through a month of stories that brought back a lot of memories for me – stories about a serial killer in the northwest who was stalking college co-eds (the killer was later identified as Ted Bundy), the withdrawal of American soldiers from Vietnam, the Watergate scandal. And through the month of July, 1974, I tried to picture Thom Bishop – still alive then, moving and breathing and laughing, unaware that his short time here was coming to a close.

I moved on to August, 1974.

The story was brief. Thom Bishop climbed a utility pole, was electrocuted, fell from the pole, and sustained a head injury from which he died several days later.

I was surprised, to say the least. In all my fantasies about my friend, Thom – he'd become my friend over the months I'd been sitting on his bench – I'd never expected this.

I returned the microfiche to the librarian, and, on impulse, asked her if the library had any yearbooks from local high schools. She was able to find one for the school Thom had attended during the time he'd been there. I looked up his name in the index and turned to the page listed. Thom's photo showed a bespectacled teenager with a sweet grin and a mop of curly hair. I smiled when I saw his picture. Now I actually knew what my friend looked like.

Today I sat on his bench once more. Read again the words on the plaque in front of me. "Grounded before he could soar." Oh lord. Now that I knew how Thom had died, I found myself chuckling wryly, and with a certain affection for Thom, at the irony in those words.

I never had a chance to know Thom while he was here. I really wish I had. I think he and I would have been great buds. And I'm really grateful to him for providing me with a bench to sit on and a mystery to be solved. I hope someday I will meet Thom, and I'll be able to thank him for the joy "getting to know him" brought to my life.

***

Just about the time *Blessings: Adventures of a Madcap Christian Scientist* went to print, my Aunt Elsie passed on. I was really glad that, before she passed, Elsie had been able to see the rough draft for the book, and had seen that I'd dedicated it to her, and Aunt Junie, and my mom.

The drive down to say good-bye to Elsie while she was still with us in body was very intense for me. In *Blessings* I mention a drive I was on with my young sons to see my aunts, and I mention a car accident that I witnessed – I pulled over to help the young woman involved. That accident had happened on my drive to Portland, Oregon, to say good-bye to Elsie.

I'd never seen a dying person before, and I wasn't sure what to expect. I was a little nervous about it. But I found that the sight of Aunt Elsie wasn't scary or disturbing to me in any way. She was unconscious when I arrived at her home, and, other than her labored breathing, she looked to be asleep.

Other family members were there to say good-bye, too. We made a kind of loose circle around her and we each said good-bye to her in our own way. For me, this involved singing. I held Elsie's hand and sang one of my favorite hymns in the *Christian Science Hymnal* – Hymn #412 – the melody is *Londonderry Air*, the words were written by Rosa M. Turner:

> *O dreamer, leave thy dreams for joyful waking,*
> *O captive, rise, and sing, for thou art free;*
> *The Christ is here, all dreams of error breaking,*
> *Unloosing bonds of all captivity,*
> *He comes to bless thee on his wings of healing;*
> *To banish pain, and wipe all tears away;*
> *He comes anew, to humble hearts revealing*
> *The mounting footsteps of the upward way.*
>
> *He comes to give thee joy for desolation,*
> *Beauty for ashes of the vanished years;*
> *For every tear to bring full compensation,*
> *To give thee for confidence for all thy fears.*
> *He comes to call the dumb to joyful singing;*
> *The deaf to hear; The blinded eyes to see,*
> *The glorious tidings of salvation bringing.*
> *O captive, rise, thy Saviour comes to thee.*

There were a couple moments as I sang to her that it seemed to me, and the others who were with us, that Elsie wanted to join me in song. Her lips moved, and sound came from her mouth. Of course I can't say, for sure – but I like to think that she was singing with me one last time before she left us.

Mary Baker Eddy admonishes us in *Science and Health* to "never record ages" – but I feel the need to mention that Elsie was 94 when she died. She'd spent most of her life as a practicing Christian Scientist, and had relied almost exclusively on Christian Science for healing during those years.

And even at the age of 94, those unfamiliar with Christian Science seemed to blame her death on Christian Science. There was some head-shaking going on amongst the dear care-givers and I overheard one of them say, "She's a Christian Scientist," as if that explained why she was dying.

Ahem. Did I mention that Elsie was 94 when she died?

***

I am tempted to put quotation marks around "died" whenever I type it. I use that word loosely, I guess, because I don't really know what it means. I mean, I know it marks the end of life – but does life ever really end? For that matter, does it ever really begin? Is there ever really any birth *or* death? I don't think I've ever actually died before, so I don't know, for sure, what happens after "death." I'm quite sure, though, that we aren't borne off to literal places of "hell" and "heaven" when we die – Christian Science teaches that heaven and hell are states of mind, not actual places – and that we carry heaven and hell around within our thoughts – when we're full of joy, hope, and love we're in heaven, and when we're full of fear, anger, and hate we're in hell – and we don't need to die to experience either one. As Jesus said, "The kingdom of God is within you."

The idea of death – of all the energy, thoughts, and love that are the essence of an individual just disappearing – has never made sense to me... I just can't wrap my thoughts around the idea of it. It doesn't compute. From my perspective, there's a purpose to life, a reason for being – to love, and learn, and be part of something infinitely wonderful – and it doesn't make sense, then, for all that we're learning here, for all the progress we're making as individuals, to just come to an end.

Maybe the good thoughts we send out and the good in our lives continues on in some kind of collective, communal wave towards good...? I don't know. Maybe in my Golden Years book I'll have more insight about it all.

Suffice it to say, I don't believe all the intelligence, humor, and courage that was the essence of Elsie can die, really. I believe Elsie continues on.

***

Several years after Elsie passed on, I got the call that my beloved Aunt Junie was dying. This was a really hard one for me. Junie had been a huge support to me the year before, during TYoI. I don't know how I would have made it through that time without her loving confidence in me.

I talked to Junie on the phone just a week before I got the call that she was dying. There was one thing that really surprised me during this conversation: Junie said she couldn't understand why everyone was taking such good care of her - she didn't think she deserved everything that people were doing for her. I was shocked!!! I told her that she deserved everything and more - that she'd given us all so much! But she was just really surprised by all the kind care. Isn't that weird?! I think people don't always realize the impact they have on other peoples' lives.

As always, her humor made me laugh, and the love I felt coming through the phone seemed almost tangible. We kept telling each other that we loved each other. I was wondering – and I'm pretty sure she was wondering, too – if this would be the last time we'd ever talk to each other here.

***

As with Aunt Elsie, Junie was unconscious when we arrived at the hospice care center she was staying in. As I'd done with Aunt Elsie, I sang to Junie and held her hand, and tried to wrap her up in my love for her. I didn't want to let her go. I felt she was with us, that she could still hear us. We all told her how much we loved her. Mom said she's sure she saw Junie smile.

After everyone had left the room, I had to go back – I just wanted to have one last moment alone with Junie, to tell her I loved her without it being a show for anyone else, if that makes sense. But when I returned to her room, I felt that she'd left – that she'd already moved on. I think – and, of course, this is just sheer speculation on my part – but, I think that Junie had stayed with us until we all could say good-bye to her, and once we'd done that – once her baby sister, my mom, had arrived and said good-bye – I think Junie felt she could leave then.

I'm so grateful that I was able to talk with her the week before, and I'm so grateful that I was able to travel down to say good-bye to her. I know Junie would not want anyone to get all maudlin and weepy about her departure – she would have told us all to "Get a grip, for Pete's sake!" And I've tried to do that for her. But it ain't always been easy.

***

One of the best gifts Junie left me after her passing was the opportunity to reconnect to my female cousins – Junie's nieces. In the years since Junie's death we've reconnected to spread her ashes over the Pacific, to share her inheritance, and to just get together and laugh and learn from each other. Our Aunt Junie was special and precious to each of us, and, as we've shared our stories, I've come to realize what a positive influence she was in each of our lives.

Around Christmas, my cousin, Julie, invited all her family and friends to join her in a celebration of life. Julie is a trooper – a courageous, loving woman who has been challenged by recent radiation and chemotherapy treatments, and has shared with us all that she's learned about life from her experiences confronting death. And how wonderful it was to come together with Julie and my other cousins, and all the people who are special in Julie's life, to celebrate with her. In the Christmas letter she sent us after her celebration, she wrote: "Yes, during this Christmas season I know what it is to be joyful. We've heard that 'love is all there is'. True. True. In this past year the embrace of family and friends, the ability to openly express and receive love - what a gift! What a treasure! And so to each of you… whatever is happening in your life… whatever challenges you face… I wish for love to be present. Because nothing… *really* nothing… can overwhelm the beauty, grace and contentment found in the spirit of love."

***

I believe that Junie continues to progress and work out "the great problem of being" (a phrase used by Mary Baker Eddy), and I believe that one day we will be able to laugh with each other once again.

***

There are still things I'm "working on" in Christian Science – I've been working on the problem of near-sightedness for years, for instance – but I don't blame Christian Science for still being myopic – blaming Christian Science for my myopia, would be like me blaming the principles of mathematics if I couldn't figure out the answer to an algebra problem. The principles of mathematics have already provided me with the solutions, and it's up to me to work the problems out. I believe Christian Science has provided me with the solutions, too – and it's up to me to work out my problems by learning how to use those principles correctly.

I suppose if traditional medical science could guarantee it would cure its adherents 100% of the time, and never harm or kill them while it was trying to cure them, there'd be no reason to go anywhere else for help with bodily illness. But, of course, medical science can't make those guarantees – it's not an exact science, like physics, with consistent, dependable principles – sometimes it works, sometimes it doesn't, sometimes what helps one person in medical science, may actually end up killing someone else, and – as is often the case in cancer treatment, for instance – sometimes the treatment can be as debilitating, painful, and harmful, in the end, as the original problem it was supposed to fix. Maybe it shouldn't be surprising that people sometimes seek alternatives to it.

There's no denying that, just as people often die while under medical treatment, people have died while under Christian Science treatment, too. It's even possible that at some point *I* will appear to die (I know – hard to believe, right? But I think we need to consider the small possibility that I might not, after all, ascend), and it's possible that I will be under Christian Science treatment when that happens. And I really, really hope that *if* I should appear to die, my loved ones will not blame Christian Science for this – I hope my loved ones will be able to recognize that Christian Science helped make me the person they love and that there was something in me – maybe a part of me they love – that was drawn to this way of life.

I think we need to allow every individual his or her own life experience. I know it may be hard sometimes to watch those we love make choices regarding their lives and health when we don't understand, or don't agree with, those choices. But I believe we need to allow our loved ones to live their lives with integrity, and give them the respect and freedom to make their own decisions when it comes to their health, and their lives.

For me, Christian Science is so much more than some kind of alternative health care system. Christian Science is a way of looking at the world, and it's a way of life. Physical healing is just a nice side-effect of striving to live life as a pure expression of Love, Truth, and Life – of God.

Children of the Belay

Blest be the tie that binds
Our hearts in Christian love;
The fellowship of kindred minds
Is like to that above.

When we asunder part,
It gives us inward pain;
But we shall still be joined in heart,
And hope to meet again.
- John Fawcett

***

(The story of the COB get-together was first told in *Newsweek*'s on-line *My Turn* column, on November 2, 2006.)

In my first book, *Blessings: Adventures of a Madcap Christian Scientist*, I shared the story of the 1953 expedition to K2 that my father had been a part of, and I talked about the belay (a technique climbers use to stop another climber from falling by winding the climbing rope around a secure object) that had saved my dad's life, and the lives of four other men on that expedition. Because I was born a good three years after *The* Belay (as it's come to be known in the annals of climbing history), I had always been personally grateful to Pete Schoening, the man who had been responsible for The Belay. Not only had Pete saved the lives of the five falling men, but he'd also made it possible for those men to return home and have children. I wrote: "I've often thought of the children born to these men at least nine months after this expedition as the 'Children of the Belay' and, although I've never met all the other spawn of these adventurers, I feel a certain connection to them."

Through the years I'd sometimes thought about the other descendants of the K2 expedition – all of them impacted as I had been by that moment when those five men had been pulled back from the brink of death. I wondered if the other climbers' kids felt the same gratitude to Pete that I did. Had their fathers, like mine, introduced them to the joys of the great outdoors? Would we feel the same instant bonds of friendship that our fathers had felt, if we ever met?

In 2005, at Pete's memorial service, I found that his children shared my desire to meet our fellow "Children of the Belay" or "COB" (as I'd dubbed the K2 climbers' descendants). Soon e-mails were flying from one COB to the next and the idea of a COB get-together began to become a reality. Finally, in August of 2006, 28 descendants of the expedition members – coming from Germany, New York, Colorado, New Mexico, and Washington State – along with spouses and partners, my dad, and the widows of George Bell and Pete Schoening, converged on the small town of Leavenworth, Washington, to have our COB Get-Together.

***

As my family pulled into Leavenworth we saw Kim Schoening's husband standing on the sidewalk outside the Forest Service Station and he waved us into the parking lot. The lot was bursting with lively, laughing COB. There was George Bell's daughter, Carolyn, and his son, George, Jr. And there were Pete's children: Kim, Kristiann, Mark, Lisa, and Eric. I'd never met the Bell offspring until now, but without hesitation I found myself getting out of the car and introducing myself to them, shaking Carolyn's hand and giving George a hug. It was like we were old friends meeting again after a long separation.

On a hike through the woods to Icicle Creek, we chatted and learned the basics about one another: Jobs, hometowns, educations. Afterwards we ate lunch at a restaurant and then splashed and swam around in the Wenatchee River. There was a young lad there with a skimboard and we took turns trying to stay upright on the thing. (To be honest, the second generation COB seemed more adept at this than us firstlings.) Later we celebrated one of the grand-COB's birthdays, singing *The Birthday Song* in honor of her nineteenth year.

But for me the standout experience came that night as we watched a BBC video on the K2 Expedition. When Pete Schoening's face appeared on the screen a little voice excitedly piped up, "There's Grampa!" And it hit me that for the first time in my life I was in a room full of people who could relate to the story of the expedition in the same way that I relate to it. Here were other spawn of those adventurers, as familiar with the personalities and events of the expedition as I was. As we watched the videos, we all laughed in the same places, and shared the same respect for the courage and camaraderie shown by the climbers. Even the littlest children listened quietly.

The next morning was Sunday and we decided to hold a church service in the yurt on the property we'd invaded for the weekend. Pete and Dad had not been religious men, but both married Christian Scientists, and George Sr.'s mother-in-law had been one, so we decided to pattern the service after a Christian Science service as that was familiar to many of us. The yurt had this huge, round window at its apex, and as Pete's son, Mark, and daughter, Kim, conducted the service, I lay on my back and looked up through the window into the pine trees, and let my thoughts draw close to the beauty and peace of God, Love. There was a feeling of gratitude and joy that permeated the yurt that morning, and I was so glad to be there.

***

As we prepared to leave Leavenworth the adieus were bittersweet – although we'd only been together for two days it felt as if I was saying good-bye to family. The members of our fathers' expedition had gone into the mountains as strangers and had come out as friends. Maybe it's not surprising that the same was true for their children.

***

Probably the day after we returned from our get-together, I began to write up my recollections and reflections of the COB's time together. It had been, for me, an amazing experience to be able to meet all these other people who were connected with me by the adventure our fathers had shared more than 50 years before. Once I'd written the story, I had a need to share our happy time together with others, and the thought came to me that maybe *Newsweek* would be interested in using it in its *My Turn* column. So I emailed a copy of the story into the editors in New York.

I didn't hear from *Newsweek* for a couple months, and figured the editors had decided against using my piece. (As I recall now, I think it said in the submission guidelines that only one in, like, 600 submitted stories gets published in the *My Turn* column.) I pretty much forgot about it.

Then one day, I received a call from Joshua, one of the editors at *Newsweek*, telling me they wanted to run the story. This was followed by an email, sent to me on November 1st:

Hi Karen,
You'll find your piece attached. I have inserted queries in red. Please incorporate the questions I've asked and suggestions I've made and send them to me tonight or tomorrow morning at the latest.

As we discussed earlier, I will then send it up to another editor, who will go through and make more minor changes. When it's completely through the ringer, I'll send you another copy to take a look at and approve (via e-mail or fax, whichever is more convenient for you at work). I'll call you at the work number to discuss this.

Additionally, tomorrow I'll e-mail you a contract which you'll need to print, fill out and fax back to me. The contract is not extremely urgent, but the sooner the better (i.e. within the next couple of days). Payment for the column is $500, which you should expect to receive 6-7 weeks after the date of publication. The sooner I get the contract, the sooner we can start processing the payment.

That's it!

If you have any questions, please feel free to give me a call.

***

Newsweek?! My story was going to be published in *Newsweek*?! This was heady stuff, and, I have to admit, I was pretty puffed-up about it all.

At the time, my computer was set up right next to the woodstove (I didn't have an option to go "wireless" with my then-computer and I think it was the only place we could fit it in the house or something), and I remember sitting there, back to the stove, sweat pouring down my face as I tried to get the story ready for the *Newsweek* editors. I worked on it late into the night, and probably about midnight was able to finally send it off to them.

So – picture it – the next day I'm at the school where I was teaching, and during my lunch break a call comes through to the school secretary that a *Newsweek* editor wants to talk to me. The secretary patches the call through to me in the staffroom, and, as I'm answering final questions about the story, my principal walks into the staffroom, quickly intuits that everyone's attention is focused on me and the phone in my hand, and asks what's going on. "I'm talking to my editor at *Newsweek* in New York," I answer matter-of-factly, like this is an everyday occurrence for me. I will never forget the look on my principal's face. Priceless. Absolutely priceless.

That very day the story was published on-line. I sent off emails to all my fellows COBs to let them know we'd "gone international" and, of course, I sent off a flurry of emails to… well… pretty much everybody I'd ever met in my entire life, to let them know they could now find my by-line in, yup, *Newsweek*.

The story of the COB get-together ended up being far-reaching amongst the mountaineering community. The story was mentioned at the annual American Alpine Club meeting, and popped up in several blogs, and the picture of the COBs at their get-together even became part of a display at the Bradford Washburn American Mountaineering Museum in Golden, Colorado.

The ripples from Pete Schoening's heroic belay on K2 in 1953 continue to expand, and I'm so glad to have been able to be a part of it all.

***

In *Blessings* I talked about my friendship with Pete's daughter, Kim, and her husband, Rich. I shared how I was able to connect Kim and Rich to a young woman I knew who was pregnant, and needed to find a home for the baby she was carrying. Kim and Rich adopted the baby boy when he was born. A couple years later, Kim gave birth to another son. Kim ~d Rich's sons are the same age as our sons, and through the ve've made an effort to keep our families connected.

Several years ago, not long after Aunt Junie passed on, I received unexpected word from Kim's mom that Kim had passed on.

Just as with Aunt Junie, and just as with Aunt Elsie, I believe that Kim's life continues on – the exuberance, joy, and generosity that were qualities so beautifully expressed by Kim, simply can't be extinguished. I really believe that.

After Kim's passing it maybe became even more important to me that our sons keep their connection to each other. And so, last summer, when we were visiting Scott's family on the east coast, we gave a call to Rich, who lives about an hour from Scott's folks' home. Rich and his sons drove to meet us and we spent a day together, swimming in Lake Sacandaga, and chatting about life.

And to see these four handsome, intelligent young men – brought together and connected to each other by The Belay – laughing with each other, and talking about universities, and their future plans – really touched my heart and brought tears to my eyes.

Kim's mom has often talked about "the ties that bind" – and these young men are proof of those ties.

Starting Over

"No man also seweth a piece of new cloth on an old garment: else the new piece that filled it up taketh away from the old, and the rent is made worse. And no man putteth new wine into old bottles else the new wine doth burst the bottles, and the wine is spilled, and the bottles will be marred: but new wine must be put into new bottles." – Mark 2: 21-22

"Willingness to become as a little child and leave the old for the new, renders thought receptive of the advanced idea. Gladness to leave the false landmarks and joy to see them disappear, - this disposition helps to precipitate the ultimate harmony." – Mary Baker Eddy

"We must be willing to let go of the life we've planned, so as to have the life that is waiting for us. The old skin has to be shed before the new one can come." – Joseph Campbell

***

I had been becoming increasingly unhappy in my career. I found myself in a position in which the things that had given me great joy from my profession – the opportunity to engage young people in creative lessons and learning, the energy, spontaneity, and fun – were no longer a part of my job.

On one of my walks one day just before the beginning of the new school year, I ran into Punky, owner of the local pre-school. She was in her yard, getting it ready for her granddaughter's wedding. She was covered in dirt, wearing her work clothes, and, as always, she looked beautiful.

I don't think Punky and I had ever talked before about my job as a teacher. And I'm not sure how the subject came up this time – I probably brought it up because it'd been a lot on my mind lately. I shared with her the most recent experiences with my school district, and my sadness and disappointment with the direction education, in general, seems to be headed. Then she shared some of *her* stories with the current educational system, and for a moment we stood there together, shaking our heads in our mutual sadness about it all.

Finally Punky looked up at me from her reverie and searched my face for a moment. Then she said something that brought unexpected tears to my eyes. "God is forcing you to move on. He has other plans for you." It was a statement of fact, the way Punky said it. And I knew she was right.

I'd known for a while that I was approaching the time when I'd need to move on. I'd had a good career, it was a marvelous era for me, and it was the right place for me at the time - but I knew in my heart that I was nearing the end of that era, and that soon there would come a day when I would know I was supposed to be doing something else.

***

I held on for a few more months. During that time I was led to meet with my financial advisor – a man I hadn't talked to for years – and, instead of laughing at my desire to leave my career, he gave me some really helpful suggestions, and helped set in motion some financial changes that would prove to be important in a few months, though I didn't know that at the time.

I kept listening for God's direction – trusting Him to show me what to do, and when to do it. Mary Baker Eddy writes in *Science and Health*: "When the ocean is stirred by a storm, then the clouds lower, the wind shrieks through the tightened shrouds, and the waves lift themselves into mountains. We ask the helmsman: 'Do you know your course? Can you steer safely amid the storm?' He answers bravely, but even the dauntless seaman is not sure of his safety; nautical science is not equal to the Science of Mind. Yet, acting up to his highest understanding, firm at the post of duty, the mariner works on and awaits the issue. Thus should we deport ourselves on the seething ocean of sorrow. Hoping and working, one should stick to the wreck, until an irresistible propulsion precipitates his doom or sunshine gladdens the troubled sea."

And so I continued "hoping and working" and, when the "irresistible propulsion" came, I recognized it and knew, absolutely knew, the time had come to "leave the old for the new. "

***

Even though I had no doubt it was time to start over, my rebirth into a new life did not come without some struggle. As I ended one life and began a new one, a second bout of depression hit me – but this time it was caused entirely by extrinsic factors, rather than intrinsic ones – and this time I was better prepared to deal with it.

Once again, my community of friends and family lifted me up.

I emailed David Allen again, this time asking him if he'd ever felt like a loser. And, as before, his words touched me, and played a huge part in giving me the assurance I needed about myself right then:

> *"Yes, sometimes I feel like a loser. Sometimes, I AM a loser. Sometimes, I am a winner. Most of the time, I am somewhere in-between. Our lives have a frequency like a wave of water. When I feel like a loser and I am down in that deep trough, I just remind myself that I will soon be on the way back up to the peak of the wave. And, pretty soon, I am. You and I have both lived long enough to know that...But let me make one thing perfectly clear: You, Karen, are an awesomely cool person. You are kind, compassionate, generous, lovely. You are a great mom, wife, sister, daughter, teacher, mentor, advocate, and many other wonderful things. I admire you and learn from you. You are not a loser. Sometimes you might feel like a loser, but that doesn't change the reality of who you are and what you mean to the people in your life. You are loved by many people. I really mean that."*

How can I tell you what David's encouraging and generous words meant to me just then? David had given me the exactly right thoughts I needed, and his affirmation of me as "loved" helped lift me from a place of self-condemnation and misery.

I think if all of mankind were able to recognize the good in themselves and in each other – I think this, alone, would transform our world.

My brother, Pete, soon sent me an email that bolstered me up, too. He wrote, in part: "You have one of the finest lives I have seen anyone live. You are loved and admired by many people. I love you so much. I have always looked up to you for how to live a life. You have always been the strong one of us three. I believe you still are."

Chip, a wonderful man in Florida who had read my book, and tracked me down, and whom I now felt blest to count among my friends, always seemed to send me messages full of kindness and compassion, at exactly the right time – it was like he was somehow tuned into my feelings.

And my neighbor, Peggy, daily left me little notes about how much I'd meant to her children as their teacher – every day she had a new memory from one of them that she shared with me. She also got me "out there" during a time when I needed someone to do that – invited me to listen to her son's folk-rock-jazz band perform at a local restaurant, invited me over to learn how to weave on her loom, and invited me to come to be part of the fellowship, and all the doings, at the local community hall. Another neighbor, Diane, invited me to meet with her sewing group and told me I could use her humongous crafts room whenever I wanted to sew and create. My church family learned something of my situation and, during a meeting which I didn't attend, voted to pay me a small salary every month to serve as their Reading Room librarian – this provided me with one day a week when there was structure to my day, when I could feel that I had some purpose – and the fact that my little church was willing to pay me, even a small salary, for doing this, meant a great deal to me.

There are so many people – former colleagues and fellow Christian Scientists, neighbors, and former students, and family members, and internet friends – who enveloped me in their love and kept me going. I was really amazed and overwhelmed by their outpouring of kindness and encouragement. I felt wealthy beyond description.

***

I recently went to a workshop on "form" and "essence" given by a local life coach named Laura Lavigne – ~~rgetic~~, dynamic woman whom my financial advisor (of ~~had~~ recommended I meet. I'd never done any kind of life coach stuff before, and wasn't sure what to expect. I was a little skeptical, to tell you the truth. But oh my goodness! The thoughts that Laura shared with us that day were really eye-opening and enlightening. Laura talked about the "form" being the physical something that represents the "essence." A couch, for instance, might be a form for "comfort." Laura pointed out that when we talk with each other, we usually talk in terms of "form" rather than "essence." We ask each other, "Do you want the red shoes or the blue shoes?" When what we might actually be asking each other is what it is we want to feel: "What will those red shoes do for you? And how will that make you feel?" We limit ourselves to the forms, rather than focusing on the essences we want in our lives. And in doing that, we limit ourselves to the forms with which we're already familiar, and close ourselves up to the infinite possibilities of the other forms we don't even know about. To illustrate this, Laura drew a big circle on the whiteboard and cut out a quarter of it – "This is what we know," Laura said. She cut out another quarter – "This is what we know we don't know." The remaining half of the circle? "This," she said, "is what we don't know we don't know. This is where the magic is."

    I love that!

    In his book, *Lectures and Articles on Christian Science,* Edward Kimball writes, "It is probable that there will come a time when you will be in quest of professional or business occupation; when you will be in want of a situation. Let us assume that you will be entitled to it and that it will be right for you to be employed righteously and profitably. Such an assumption as this carries with it scientifically the conclusion that if it is right for you to have such a thing, that thing must be in existence and must be available…One of the most influential human conditions is the one which I will call expectancy…You are entitled to the fullness and ampleness of life, but you will need to learn that gloomy foreboding never solves a problem and never releases the influences that make for your largest prosperity and advantage."

Good isn't a miracle. It is natural for us to have good in our lives – we shouldn't be surprised by it. We should expect good.

I'm still not sure, exactly, what form the future will take for me, but I know what the essence of it will be. I know there will be freedom, joy, purpose, love, and laughter. Those things can't be denied me, and they are not dependent on a specific form. The freedom, joy, purpose, love, and laughter that I have now, and are always available to me, can't be measured, limited, confined or restricted. The future holds boundless possibilities - for me, and for you, too.

Never a Dull Moment

"There are no ordinary moments" – Dan Millman, from *The Peaceful Warrior.*

"How wonderful it is that nobody need waste a single moment before starting to improve the world." – Anne Frank

***

So what, you may be wondering, have I been doing in the months since I "started over"?

Well, let's see... got the tires rotated, and took the car in for a tune-up, pruned my roses, planted some flowers, mowed the lawn, made a lot of dinners for my family, did laundry, washed dishes, vacuumed, dusted, and swept, organized the pantry, cleaned out the garage and took stuff to the Goodwill, worked in the Reading Room, sang a solo at church, made appointments, went to appointments, attended meetings, went on a lot of walks, visited Mom and Dad a couple times, started three blogs, sold my first photo notecard, and then another, and another, and a couple more, had a story published in the local paper and on my alma mater's website, wrote a book, wrote another book, met a cool life coach, made a vision board, began weaving a scarf, went to Xander's track meets, went to the district caucus, became a delegate to the county convention, became a delegate to the state convention, walked in a march to protest coal trains, walked in a march to support farm-workers, wrote letters to senators, representatives, and the governor about education reform, did contract editing on supplements for an educational publisher, and edited my dad's autobiography. For starters.

Oh my goodness – there is always something useful to do, isn't there?

When I first left my job, I was a little scared about what it was going to look like for me, and for my family. I worried that we might not be able to survive financially, and I worried that I wouldn't have purpose to my days.

I'm not worried anymore. I know that every moment we are provided with what we need – I've seen evidence of this.

And here's an interesting thing: I've discovered that it actually cost me, financially, to work in a position that was not the right fit for me. I've never had extravagant tastes – but I have to admit that when I was stressed and unhappy in my job, I'd find myself buying things I didn't really need – baubles and doodads and googaws for the house, career clothing and shoes, and vacations to try to escape from my life. I no longer feel the need to buy baubles, doodads and googaws, career clothing, or "escape" vacations.

I think The Middle Book is just about done now.

The Beginning

"The very circumstance, which your suffering sense deems wrathful and afflictive, Love can make an angel entertained unawares." – Mary Baker Eddy

*"For life, with all its yields of joy or woe
And hope and fear,
Is just our chance o' the prize of learning love –
How love might be, hath been, indeed, and is."*
- Elizabeth Browning

"There's nothing in a caterpillar that tells you it's going to be a butterfly."
- Richard Buckminster Fuller

***

Isn't it great to be alive?!

Four years ago I wasn't sure I was going to make it to today. Think back on the last four years of your life, my friend – become aware of all the things you would have missed if you'd given up on life four years ago: the new friends you would never have known; the sunsets and sunrises you wouldn't have seen; the lessons you wouldn't have learned; the changes you wouldn't have been able to make; the pictures never painted; the photos never taken; the songs never sung; all the love and laughter that you would have denied yourself.

Kind of mind-boggling, isn't it?

I am so glad you and I didn't give up on life.

When I was deep into the depression, I couldn't imagine a happy ending to my story. I couldn't imagine I'd ever get out of it, and couldn't imagine it ever ending. I was really scared that I was going to spend the rest of my life like that, and I didn't think I'd make it.

I remember days when I'd be at work and I'd just keep saying "Thank you, God. Thank you, God. Thank you, God…" under my breath, trying to get from one moment to the next, and thanking God with each breath for that moment, before I had to face the next one – sort of like those moments between contractions in childbirth, when a woman steels herself for the next series of pains.

I still have moments of loneliness, and I still have moments when I'm scared. But now I know enough to know these moments will eventually pass. I don't give much thought to them. I've discovered it's possible to be happy even during these times.

And drats. I have just had an epiphany:

In her review of my book, *Blessings: Adventures of a Madcap Christian Scientist*, Rosemary Thornton wrote, "I've not yet met a woman who's lived more than 40 years on this earth, who doesn't have quite a few items in the 'I don't understand this' file. I'd love to have read a few stories – written in Ms. Terrell's delightful style and voice – that didn't have perfect and tidy endings." I really wanted to give Ms. Thornton a book filled with loose ends and a bunch of untidy endings. I have tried. I really have. I've been rushing to get this book done before The Golden Years come, so that there'd be some kind of cliff-hanger here, and loose ends galore, and you'd all be waiting in suspense to see what happens to the Madcap Christian Scientist next.

And I just realized that I've been in the Golden Years all along!

I know. I am incorrigible.

obtained at www.ICGtesting.com